KIDNAPPED!
AT CHOWCHILLA

by
Gail Moock Miller
and
Sandra Tompkins

Logos International
Plainfield, New Jersey

KIDNAPPED! AT CHOWCHILLA
Copyright © 1977 by Logos International
Printed in the United States of America
All rights reserved
International standard book number: 0-88270-217-3
Library of Congress catalog card number: 76-56699
Published by Logos International
Plainfield, New Jersey 07061

"Our children have been kidnapped!"

Jennifer and Jeffrey were not home from school yet when their mother returned from work that steamy July afternoon. Her calls for the children echoed through empty rooms. Where were those children? Was the school bus late?

In other homes throughout the drowsy little community of Chowchilla, California, parents watched for children who were late. Had the school bus broken down enroute from the school? Parents, police, and school officials combed the highways. For the waiting parents, minutes turned to hours and irritation to anxiety, and then panic.

At last the school bus was found, cleverly camouflaged—and empty. For the stunned parents of twenty-six small children, an unbelievable nightmare had only begun.

For the children, terror had invaded their world in the midafternoon when two masked men forced their way onto their bus. They were jammed tightly into smaller vehicles, covered suffocatingly with canvas, and for eleven hours they cried, prayed, and begged their captors to release them. When the vans finally stopped it was to force the small victims into a hole in the floor of a quarry where they were buried alive.

What faith sustained those children during the ensuing seventeen hours before they finally clawed their way out of what could have been their mass grave? How did a stricken community find new faith in the jaws of catastrophe? Here is the complete story by two area reporters who covered first-hand the events of those two terrifying days when all over the world people went to their knees to plead for the lives of twenty-six children.

To all the people who believed God would bring a bus driver and twenty-six school children home safely.

ACKNOWLEDGMENTS

We express our thanks to the families of the children involved in the kidnapping, who shared with us their innermost feelings during a most painful time in their lives.

A special thank you to our families who sacrificed their own comfort so we could follow the Lord's leading as we wrote this book: Scott Tompkins and John and Scott Miller.

Special notes to Desa C. Belyea, Sunday editor of *The Fresno Bee* for editing the book; to Kathy Hickingbottom and Jean Gatewood for their guidance and prayers; to Winston and Joy Handwerker for fruitful work sessions at their mountain home; to Linda Tuggle and Marsha Palmateer for taking care of Scotty.

THE VICTIMS

Lisa Ardery, 9	Jodie Heffington, 10
Monica Ardery, 5	Sherry Hinesley, 7
Lisa Barletta, 12	Mike Marshall, 14
Jeffrey Brown, 10	Jody Matheny, 10
Jennifer Brown, 9	Andrea Park, 8
Irene Carrejo, 12	Larry Park, 6
Julia Carrejo, 7	Barbara Parker, 8
Linda Carrejo, 8	Becky Reynolds, 9
Stella Carrejo, 6	Judy Reynolds, 13
Darla Daniels, 9	Angela Robison, 10
Johnny Estabrook, 8	Michelle Robison, 11
Andres Gonzales, 8	Cindy Van Hoff, 7
Roberto Gonzales, 11	Laura Yazzie, 8

Bus Driver Frank "Edward" Ray, 55

(Ages accurate at the time of the kidnapping)

INTRODUCTION

The nation was on its knees.

Coast to coast the news services flashed bulletins of the mysterious kidnapping of twenty-six school children and their bus driver from their school bus in a small farming community in central California. It was Thursday, July 15, 1976.

Within hours, the name "Chowchilla" was on the lips of millions of people who could scarcely comprehend the magnitude and horror of such a crime.

Whether alone, in prayer groups or in churches, compassionate people across the country and beyond begged God to have mercy.

The long hours until the children returned safe tested the strength and faith of the families and the children.

This is their story.

KIDNAPPED!
AT CHOWCHILLA

CHAPTER ONE

"Yoo-hoo! I'm ho-o-ome! Jeffrey? Jennifer? Where are you? Come on, you guys. I know you're hiding. Don't play games with me now."

Joan Brown looked in all their usual hiding places.

"I'm on my way into town. We're going to eat dinner out, you'd better hurry up," she called. Still, no answer.

Something was wrong. What was it? Then she noticed. The peanut butter wasn't out. There were no chairs in front of the television.

She looked at the clock. It was five. Where could they be?

She picked up the phone and called the bus driver, Ed Ray. No answer. He wasn't home yet. Joan called Lee Roy Tatom, the superintendent at

Dairyland School, and talked to his wife, Delma.

"The bus broke down along the way and the driver is not allowed to leave the bus," Delma reassured her. "Lee Roy is out checking on it."

Joan Brown sat down to wait.

Connie Hinesley looked out the window expectantly. The table was set with cookies and milk. She checked her watch again. Where was that granddaughter of hers anyway?

Sherry was usually right on time, bubbling over with the details of her day. She glanced out the window again.

Her eye caught the time on the kitchen clock: 5:15.

"Five-thirty. What could have happened to Johnny?" Jim Estabrook asked his wife, Leanna.

"I dunno. Usually he's walking in the door right at four-thirty."

Estabrook felt uneasy and walked down to the corner to see if the bus had been by. The fellow at the gas station said he hadn't seen it yet today.

Back home, Estabrook called Dairyland School. The words were reassuring: "Someone's out checking on it right now. They probably had a flat tire or broke down somewhere along the way."

Still, something didn't seem quite right.

Carol Marshall was angry. It was 5:45 and Mike wasn't home yet. She thought about their fight that morning and decided he must have gone to a friend's house just to make her worry. Or maybe he was walking home so he wouldn't have to ride the bus. He's not supposed to walk, she thought. I'm going to wring his scrawny neck when I get hold of him.

She jumped in the pickup, getting more aggravated by the minute. She had a thousand things to do to get the family's motor home ready to leave Sunday for Ogden, Utah, where they were going to meet her husband, Bob. He was the world champion steer wrestler in 1973 and tonight he was appearing in a rodeo in Calgary, Alberta, Canada.

She hoped he would do well. He was already some 5,000 points ahead of his closest competition for the world championship this year.

Carol drove along the bus route looking for Mike. He should be pretty close to home by now, she thought.

Nothing. It was after six when she returned home. The place looked deserted with Bob in Canada, Mike not home and daughter Kandi at a church camp at Jackass Rock.

The Marshalls have seventeen acres alongside Highway 152, with fifteen acres leased out in alfalfa. The small, worn house sits right on the highway and hour after hour, day and night, giant trucks roll past, drowning out conversation and threatening to flatten the house by the force of the wind.

Carol Marshall reached for the phone and called her friend, Anita Hansen, the secretary at Dairyland School.

"We've lost a bus," Anita told her.

"What do you mean, you've lost a bus?" Carol asked in disbelief.

"Don't worry about it. Edward's just broken down someplace and Lee Roy's out looking for them. We've notified the sheriff's office and the highway patrol."

"Did you see Mike get on the bus?" Carol asked. "He was supposed to, but I'm not sure he did."

"I saw him. He got on the bus. There's nothing you can do, just wait," Anita told her.

Bob Reynolds paced back and forth across the living room. His daughters, Judy and Becky, were more than an hour late from summer school and all the school office could tell him was that the bus had probably broken down.

Not content to wait at home, he told his wife, Evelyn, he was going out to look for the bus. That way, the middle-aged mechanic reasoned, if the bus had broken down, he could be of some help.

He was not the only one out looking for the bus.

Lee Roy Tatom was just walking in the door when his home phone rang. His son, Brent, answered it. "Ed Ray's bus is late," he said.

Tatom called the school to ask, "Where's Edward?"

"He's not in yet." It was 4:45 P.M.

Then, he called the Chowchilla Police Department, but one of the parents had already notified them. They, in turn, had notified the Madera County Sheriff's Department.

Sheriff's Sgt. William L. Cooley was out in the patrol car when the call came in. He dispatched officers Chuck Reiring and Steve Whitney to Chowchilla, then headed there himself.

Tatom and Truitt Dixon, another bus driver, met at the school, then split up and began zigzagging over Chowchilla's roads. The streets all run north-south and east-west with orderly names like Avenue 18, Avenue 18½, Avenue 19, or Road 14, Road 14½, Road 15.

Rather than follow the bus route exactly, Tatom first drove down the roads in the center so he could look two or three miles to the left and right and perhaps, spot the bus more quickly. All the roads are level and a big, yellow school bus would certainly stand out, Tatom figured.

When that produced no bus, he began retracing the bus's route that afternoon, all fifty-three miles of it. Still, nothing.

When Sgt. Cooley arrived in Chowchilla, he

began retracing the bus route also. He learned from Tatom that the entire route had been covered but the bus still had not been located.

Something's up, Cooley was thinking. And it will be dark soon. He issued an all-points bulletin for the missing bus and decided to get a plane in the air to see if the bus could be found. He called the dispatcher on his car radio and asked him to contact Sgt. Dennis Ring, the liaison officer between the sheriff's department and the reserve aerosquadron.

The Cessna single-engine plane was in the air by seven o'clock and began flying low over the countryside, keeping in radio communication with Cooley on the ground. Ring was accompanied by Bob Dean, a local businessman.

Suddenly, the radio communication malfunctioned. Cooley could talk to the pilot, but could not get a response.

Finally, in desperation, Cooley said, "If you can see the bus, punch your mike button twice."

"Click. Click." was the response. Then the plane dove down and dipped its wings from side to side and pulled away.

Cooley headed for the site, red lights flashing. So did the other officers, Tatom, Dixon and worried parents who were driving along the bus route.

Cooley arrived first but he still couldn't see the bus. He walked off the road, down into a slough about 150 feet. And there, hidden in tall bamboo reeds, was the school bus. It was just off Avenue

21, between Roads 15 and 16.

He had already driven by this same spot several times and never noticed the bus. It was too well hidden. Deliberately hidden.

Ordering officers Reiring and Whitney to keep the crowd of people away from the site, Cooley headed down for the bus.

His heart was in his throat. He didn't know what he might find. He knew there were at least eighteen children missing and he had read stories about people going crazy and shooting everyone in sight.

Would he find a bus full of dead bodies?

There was a deathly quiet surrounding the bus and he took a quick, deep breath before climbing aboard. He glanced around.

The bus was empty. Relief flooded over him. Yet, where did everyone go? He was certain the bus had been deliberately hidden. But why?

The possibility of kidnapping came to mind. So did UFOs. He'd heard about people being snatched, leaving not a trace. He looked around outside the bus for any clues. There, along with the bus tracks, were tracks of at least two other vehicles. He hurried back to the anxious crowd.

"The bus is empty. There's no one on it," he reported.

"What do you mean? No one on it? Where are they?" one parent demanded, starting for the bus.

"Wait! You can't go down there," Cooley said.

"Why not? My kid was on that bus and I want to see for myself."

"I can't have a bunch of people down there tramping around, destroying any evidence."

"Evidence of what? What's down there you don't want us to see?" another parent challenged.

Finally, Cooley agreed that one parent could go down to the bus with him and report back to the others. Denver Williams, stepfather of Lisa Barletta, was selected and walked obediently behind Cooley, taking care to follow the same path that had been used before.

Williams climbed aboard the bus. It was empty. He noticed a few towels, some papers, artwork. Then he reached for a ceramic ashtray Lisa had made.

"Leave it alone," Cooley ordered. "Everything has to be fingerprinted."

They left the bus and Williams confirmed everything to the others who were waiting. Cooley got on his car radio and called the Madera County Identification Bureau to send some officers immediately to comb the scene for clues: fingerprints, tire tracks, whatever they could find.

He told the office to call Sheriff Ed Bates and he would meet him at the Chowchilla police station. Bates, however, had been monitoring the radio from his home and was already on his way in.

Now Cooley had another concern. He looked at the dark sky and sensed a storm coming. He would have to get the bus out of the slough to a dry place to keep any evidence from being washed away. He ordered a large tow truck to the scene.

Cooley was starting to get excited. He knew he

was onto a big case. He'd been on the force eighteen years, but had never encountered anything like this. He is also part of the Madera County Special Emergency Reaction Team (SERT), a five-man SWAT team, and now he called other members to action.

If this was a kidnapping by some radical group, the team would have to be ready.

Carol Marshall waited at home as long as she could before getting back in the pickup and heading toward town. She decided to follow the bus route to try and find Mike.

Her thoughts raced again over this morning's argument. Mike had been in the habit of missing his bus each morning, which meant she had to drive him to school, then return to pick him up at noon. She had slept in the camper last night and come in the house to get breakfast going this morning when she realized Mike was still sleeping.

She was feeling guilty now. She had hollered and screamed, not even remembering what she said.

She told him he didn't have to go to school today or ever. Then, since it was the next to the last day, she decided he'd better make an appearance. To punish him, she said he would have to ride the bus home from school. She would not pick him up.

Her eyes tried to look for shadows along the

dusky roadside. She was sorry now.

Still no sign of life.

A crowd of people along the road caught her attention. She pulled in and jumped out of the pickup. She couldn't see the bus even though she had been driving up and down the same road several times.

"Did they find the bus?" she asked a woman standing nearby.

"Yeah."

"How are the kids?"

"The kids aren't on it," the woman answered.

Carol's mind was racing. There must have been an accident and they've already taken the kids into town.

"Where are the children?" she asked.

"We don't know."

"What do you mean, you don't know?" Her own questions were beginning to sound stupid to her.

"What do you mean you don't know?" she repeated.

"We don't know."

"Do you mean, they're not there? Where are they? Where's Ed Ray?"

CHAPTER TWO

Where are we? Where are they taking us? Why are they doing this to all these little children? Ed Ray's mind defiantly refused to quit asking questions, despite his efforts to wipe out the painful possibilities.

He squinted his eyes to make out faces in the darkness of the enclosed van. He could see Angela Robison and her sister, Michelle. They were leaning on his shoulders cramping him even tighter against the two back doors of the van. The children were nestled all around him, across his legs, chest and stomach. Some used him for a pillow, others just seemed to need the closeness, the security that he was there.

If they only knew, he thought in frustration, how shaky that security was. The drone of the engine in the van and the whine of the blower finally lulled some of the frightened children to sleep.

At least if they are asleep, they won't be so scared, Ray consoled himself. He tried to lay perfectly still so he wouldn't disturb those who were curled up around him.

Relentless questioning tore at his mind: How long would it be before the parents started looking for the children? Would anyone ever figure out what had happened?

A cramp gripped his leg like a vise and he bit his lip trying to bear the pain. He slowly moved it out from under the children. Groaning and whining cries rebelled against his movements as the sleeping children were awakened.

"Just a second!" Ray whispered. "I've got a leg cramp. Let me straighten it out."

He rubbed his aching legs and, when the pain had subsided, he gently replaced them under the children.

The exhausted bus driver lay silently staring into the darkness, straining, searching, trying to make sense out of this senseless situation.

"Oh, dear God," Ray thought to himself. "Is this for real? Are they going to murder us? All these little children?"

The day had seemed so routine. No foreboding had warned him. It had been just another sticky San Joaquin Valley day. . . .

Ed Ray looked in his rear view mirror to see that all the kids were settled in their seats. They were nosier today than usual. Must have been that swimming outing after school that had them all keyed up. Well, he could fix that fast. Ray hit the brakes and cautioned, "That's enough!" his customary warning. He had no qualms about stopping the bus altogether if they got too rowdy. But he never had to go that far. His voice was enough.

In fact, just a week ago he had separated the boys and girls—boys in front, girls in back—as punishment for their roughhousing. But here they were, carrying on again.

He couldn't help smiling as he looked back at them. Some of them looked like little drowned rats with their wet, stringy hair. Many were still wearing their wet bathing suits and he could smell the chlorine in their wet towels.

Oh well, it wouldn't be much longer. Tomorrow would be the last day of summer school and the kids were eager for vacation. So was he.

Ray pulled the bus off the road on Avenue 16 for his first stop—Edward Gregorio's house. Edward made his way through the bus, hopped down the steps and waved at his friends.

"Bye, Edward," the personable driver said, his voice drowned out by the children giving a vocal send-off to the cohort.

Ray put the big bus in gear and rolled on about another mile down the road. Just before he turned onto Road 16, he dropped off the Tripp children,

Miles, Debbie and Nancy.

Ray took a deep breath of air from the window which was opened wide next to him. But even that didn't cool him off much. The temperature was nearly a hundred degrees and the humidity almost unbearable.

Ray pulled over to let Sandy Zylstra off the bus.

"Good-bye, Edward!" she called out behind her.

"Bye now, Sandy."

Ed Ray was used to being called "Edward" by the Dairyland School children. It was an affectionate term that prevailed over the usual "Mister" accorded the other drivers. He was special to them. He had been driving a school bus for twenty-three years and, over the years, the stocky, crew-cut driver with the winning smile had come to know just about all the kids in the area. Now his bus was rolling down Road 17, past fields of alfalfa in the homestretch of this school term.

Linda Carrejo was about to burst with excitement. Today was no ordinary day. Today was *the* day.

For nearly a year, she and her girlfriends had been chasing Jeffrey Brown around at school to get his attention. And tonight she and Jeff were going to have their first date. A real honest-to-goodness date with her older sister, Irene, and her friend, Tony Werner.

Linda's brown eyes flashed a quick glance at Jeff as she took the seat across the aisle from him. He was an awfully cute boy. No question about that. Blond and stocky. And so smart!

Jeff was being so cool about their date. Just like a boy. He must be a little nervous, though, the way he kept teasing her about how scared she'd be tonight. They were going to see *Vampire Circus* at the theater downtown. Linda just giggled at his bantering.

Underneath all his teasing, Jeff was a little short on confidence himself. This was his first date and he really didn't know what he was supposed to do.

Well, he reasoned to himself, I'll just do what Tony and Irene do. But the possibilities raised by that thought shook his confidence even more.

He tried to reassure himself. You're just going to watch a movie, remember?

Mike Marshall, fourteen, was totally disinterested in the love lives of two of his juniors and sat sulking in his seat. Today was the first day he had had to ride the bus home all summer and he didn't like it one bit. He hated riding home with all these little kids. Usually his mother picked him up at school during the noon hour, but, boy, was she mad at him this morning.

Mike could still hear her screaming at him for missing the bus. He hadn't seen his mother that mad in a long, long time. He had overslept every morning the past week, regularly missing the bus so that his mother had had to drive him to school.

She did not appreciate that at all and just the day before had sprayed Mike with water to let him know how unhappy she was about the whole situation.

"I should have known better," he thought to himself.

Mike hated riding the bus from school because it took so darn long to get home.

Much as he defended his actions to himself, he couldn't help wondering if his mother would still be mad when he got home. It was punishment enough having to stay all day at summer school and here it was four o'clock in the afternoon and he was still stuck on this bus.

The bus rolled along Road 13, past corn fields, cotton fields, almond orchards and grazing dairy cattle.

Ray laughed to himself as the children on the bus tried to convince him there would be three more weeks of summer school, if they were to have their way. The school children had even gone so far as to take up a petition to present to the principal to show how badly they wanted school to continue.

Ray couldn't raise their hopes. He even bet one youngster fifty cents that tomorrow would be the last day. He knew the little guy would lose, but he also knew he'd never collect on the bet. He admired the boy's spunk and determination anyway.

He automatically turned left on Avenue 21 and in the distance he noticed a white van stopped in his lane of the road.

Mike Marshall noticed it, too, and sat up tall in his seat to look more carefully. Bet it's a road block, he thought to himself.

Probably just a breakdown, Ray decided. The guy must be having car trouble. He down-shifted the bus gears to slowly swerve around the van. He was startled by a man who jumped out in front of him, and instinctively hit the brakes.

The man had something in his hands and was yelling at Ray to stop the bus.

The man moved to the side of the bus and pointed a long-barrelled handgun through the window at Ray.

"Please open the door," the stranger commanded politely.

Ray hit the air button and the door opened.

He studied the face and weapons of the man threatening him. The face was grotesquely distorted by a nylon stocking mask. Ray saw two guns; one was a pistol, the other was a long, double-barrelled handgun. While he watched the gunman, two more armed men jumped out of the white van and climbed onto the bus.

Jeff Brown, the class cutup, responded immediately. He jumped out of his seat, raised his hands in mock fear and quipped, "We didn't do it! We didn't do it!" But this time there was no laughter at his joke.

Linda Carrejo sensed danger and immediately hid under her seat.

One of the masked strangers ordered Ray to the rear of the bus. The gunman watched Ray walk back, then he sat down in the front seat, pointing the barrel of his gun down the aisle directly at Ray.

Irene Carrejo thought a joke was being played on Ray by his friends, but when her favorite driver went to the back of the bus, she knew it was all too serious and protectively jumped up to join him in the back. She sat down in the seat in front of him.

The second man hopped into the driver's seat and put the bus in gear.

Jeff's face dropped. This was no joke.

"Ha-ha, Jeff," said his buddy, sarcastically. "Some joke!"

The children in the first three seats were commanded to move to the back of the bus by the man in front. Ed Ray was taking special notice of that square-looking protrusion from the man's shirt. A bullet-proof vest?

The bus began to roll along the country road. Ray kept his eyes intently focused on the gun aimed at him. His mind was racing. What was going on? Who were these men? What did they want? What should he do?

The emergency door! All he would have to do is pull the lever! Could he get it open without someone seeing him? If only he could drop something on the road behind them.

Just then, he heard the engine start up in the white van. It pulled in behind them. Ray didn't turn around to look, but out the side window, he could see Clarence Musick at work on his farm.

The tractor was heading toward the bus. Was this his chance? Come on Clarence, look up here! Ray silently demanded.

If only he would look up, he could see Ray riding in the back seat. He would know something was wrong. Ray's heart pounded as the tractor engine and the bus grew closer . . . and closer. . . . But just when he was near enough to notice, the farmer turned the big rig around and headed in the opposite direction.

A flush of disappointment washed over Ray. He turned his attention back to the loaded gun.

By now, the children in the bus knew there was something terribly, terribly wrong. A few started to whine and cry in fear.

Some of the braver ones asked questions. "What do you want with us? What are you doing with us? Where are you taking us?"

There were no answers. The men spoke few words—and only to each other.

Ray stared as if hypnotized at the man with the gun. One quick move by any of the kids and the captors might be jumpy enough to shoot. If only he could think of an excuse to get up to the front. He might be able to wrestle the gun away from him. Ray was strong. Years of farm work had seen to that.

A slight, muggy breeze drifted through the open windows, but it was not enough to blow away the mounting terror being experienced by the children. Six-year-old Larry Park bravely warned the kidnappers: "We'd better be home at four-thirty or somebody's going to be mad at you for takin' us!"

Turning off Avenue 21, the masked abductor pulled the bus into a thicket of bamboo twenty-feet high, growing in a dry creek bed known as Berenda Slough.

The children screamed as the bus swayed dangerously from side to side, bumping into the soft soil of the slough.

Ray looked out the window and, among the reeds, he could see another van, a dark green one, waiting.

The men ordered the children to line up. The white van was backed up to the doors of the bus so the captured children would leave no footsteps in the transfer. Eleven children were loaded into the white van. As he waited his turn, Ray strained to see the license number on the van. He said it over and over, but all he could remember were the last digits—414. He also noticed chrome rims with blue lug nuts and CB radio antennas on the center of the roof and on the right fender.

Jeff also was observing every detail he could absorb. He looked for the license plate numbers and tried to think of a way he could leave a message on the bus without letting the kidnappers know what he was doing.

When the white van was full, the doors were closed and it pulled away from the bus entrance.

Mike Marshall was packed into the front of that white van and he could hear the engine of the dark green van pulling up to the door of the bus to load the remaining passengers. Mike's stomach knotted as his terrified mind tried to imagine what was happening. What if they planned to kill the children in the other van and take his van hostage to get away?

Ray and the fifteen remaining children were loaded at gunpoint into the green van. The back doors were closed and locked.

The masked men scurried around, quickly camouflaging the hijacked bus with bamboo. The only signs left of the children on the bus were a few towels, pieces of ceramic handicraft works, pencils and papers.

The drivers climbed into the vans and slowly tried to make their way through the soft soil with their heavy cargo. The green van stuck and its tires whirred fruitlessly. A sharp streak of hope struck Ray's heart. Maybe they would stall long enough for someone to drive by! Doors opened and the abductors climbed out to investigate. He heard the door hit up against the bus. The frustrated driver quickly continued to bear down on the gas until finally there was enough momentum to move the vehicle.

Inside the white van, the young victims crowded together. Mike Marshall was the oldest and the little ones chose him to cling to immediately. Linda huddled next to Jeff. The windows in the van were paneled over and everything was covered with thick brown carpeting. They were in total darkness—a darkness that only added intensity to their fear. Poor ventilation made the air thick and stifling.

Inside the green van, conditions were even more crowded and breathing was difficult from the beginning even though there was a blower for the fifteen young passengers and Ray. They, too, had to cope with the added fear of darkness. The windows on both sides were painted white, and paneling was nailed over the rear windows.

In both vans, the victims were separated from their abductors by thick sheets of plywood, more carpeting and more paneling.

Already, many children were crying hysterically for their parents. As the kidnappers ignored their cries and the moving prison chamber bumped out of the slough, Jennifer Brown fainted in her fright.

CHAPTER THREE

In Little Jackass campground, about eighty miles from Chowchilla, Rodney Park dropped the telephone, leaving his niece's crying voice echoing from the receiver. His two children, Andrea and Larry, were dead. He knew it.

Janice Park needed only to see the expression on her husband's face to draw the same conclusion.

Mernie Murray, Rodney's sister, grabbed the phone to hear the painful details.

A niece, Sylvia Roberts, was taking care of the children in Chowchilla while Rodney, Janice and eighteen other family members had their annual camp out at Little Jackass. She had received the same nebulous information as the other parents: the children had simply vanished.

When Mernie hung up the telephone, she instinctively went to her brother's arms. They began to pray together. Each time there was a pause, she whispered firmly, "Keep praying. Keep praying."

When they finally pulled away from each other, Rodney started to make plans. They had to get home. Now. He and Janice walked back to the campground from the ranger station to tell the others what had happened. Andrea and Larry were on the missing bus.

As they turned to leave in their pickup for Chowchilla, Janice remembered that their pastor, Jerry Burns, was camping three miles up the road with a youth group from the church. She made one of Rodney's sisters promise to go there immediately to ask them to start praying. A brother and sister-in-law, Frank and Catherine, insisted on following them home.

Janice and Rodney sensed an aura of doom as they drove to Chowchilla. The cab of the pickup was as quiet as a tomb. Not a word was spoken. Throughout the long, frantic trip down the mountain, thunder and lightning flashed around them. They prayed silently, begging God to bring their children home.

"God is mad tonight," Frank said to his wife, Catherine, as he pushed on the accelerator to keep up with his brother's pickup. "God is pouring out His wrath on this town."

As they passed into the city limits, the eerie feeling grew stronger. The same thought was on all of their minds: The devil is in town tonight.

When Rodney and Janice arrived at their home on Humboldt Street, Rodney slipped into the bedroom alone and dropped to his knees to plead with God once more to bring his children home safely.

The long night was spent in tension at his brother's house listening to the raspy voices on the citizen's band radio. News of clues being found in one spot after another first encouraged, then disappointed. At one point, the electricity went off and the Parks moved outside to the car to listen from a mobile unit.

About five-thirty Friday morning, Janice telephoned her sister in Anaheim, California, to tell her the news. Her sister encouraged her to concentrate on a Scripture, Romans 8:28—"And we know that all things work together for good to them that love God, to them who are the called according to His purpose."

Throughout the ordeal, Janice held on to every word of the Scripture.

"Lord," she prayed, "you know what is best and you know why this is happening. You're the only one who knows why it's happening. But, please, give me my kids back."

Her husband was not so confident. His attitude took on a stark pessimism as he attempted to prepare himself for the worst.

"Dear God," he prayed over and over. "I know you love all little children. But please don't take mine!"

His father-in-law, Llywellen Clark, an admitted atheist, was accusing in his worry.

"Where is your God now?" he demanded.

Rodney could not answer that question. He loved his father-in-law very much, but faith in God was one thing they couldn't share.

Carol Marshall just couldn't handle this tragedy by herself. She felt so deserted and alone with Bob in Canada at the rodeo and Kandi at camp. And Mike, God only knows where Mike is, she shuddered.

Her first stop was at the house of a friend, Verlene Wood. She was anxious to share with someone the hurt, the confusion, the fear welling up inside her. Verlene always seemed so caring, so together.

Climbing out of the pickup, Carol went up and knocked at Verlene's door. No answer.

"Oh, please be home," she cried quietly. Still, no answer.

Who could she talk to? Who would understand?

She thought of Tommy Turk. He's with the sheriff's department. He could tell her what was going on up to the minute. She climbed back into the truck and realized that Tommy was at a rodeo in Salinas. She didn't know where he lived anyway.

Her next thought was Tuffy Smith. He had been on the police force and the sheriff's department. He worked closely with the law enforcement agencies and also was on the school board. If anybody could tell her anything, he could.

She arrived at Tuffy's house and found open arms to assist her.

What she heard there was only rumor—the possibility of political terrorists being behind the kidnapping—and none of it helped her to cope. The evening was spent hovering over the telephone and the television, waiting. But all she heard was other people echoing her own thoughts.

At first, Carol tried to believe that Mike had just wandered off into the slough. But Mike knew that slough like his own bedroom. If he was five years old, that may have been a possibility, but not at fourteen.

"Police still are baffled at the disappearance of twenty-six children and their bus driver from a school bus in Chowchilla late this afternoon. There are no clues. . . ."

She kept hoping something would be discovered before she had to call Bob. He would have to ride in the rodeo tomorrow and she didn't want to upset him. Bob wasn't the type to show his emotions on the outside. But inside, it would be bad.

Her mind flashed back to the deaths of several friends recently. It had been so hard to believe at the time and she knew it was true. But Mike's death. No, she refused to accept the possibility.

Finally, at one o'clock in the morning, she called Alberta, Canada, and broke the news to Bob. He would take the first plane out the next day.

Carol lay awake all night long, wondering what her husband was thinking. Sleep was out of the question. What if something happened while she was asleep? She looked around at the faces of people who were trying to overcome their own worry long enough to comfort her. They probably wouldn't wake her up anyway if it was something bad. She didn't dare close her eyes.

Like many of the others faced with this bizarre dilemma, Carol Marshall also thought about God more than she had in years.

She was uneasy in her searching for Him, primarily because of a frightening religious experience as a child. She had been forced to go to church and catechism and was frightened into believing in God. When she was old enough to refuse, she did.

But now her feelings were different. People she had never met were telling her how much they cared about her and how they were praying that the children would be returned safely.

Maybe there was something in this prayer business. It had been so long. She didn't know if she even remembered how. But if the police can't do anything and the FBI can't do anything . . . who is left?

Only God. She prayed the only prayer she could remember.

"Our Father, Who art in Heaven, hallowed be Thy name. . . ."

Jackass Rock campground was dark, except for

flashes of lightning outside. The counselors gathered around a cozy fire in the recreation center for their nightly talk. The teenagers, 126 of them, were bedded down and supposedly asleep.

The weather had been beautiful earlier in the week, but tonight a storm was raging. There were lightning and thunder and security men were checking the cabins to be sure the kids were okay.

As they talked over the next day's activities, car lights appeared from down the road.

"Who could that be at this hour?" Bertie Adams, one of the counselors, wondered out loud.

Two women came in and asked for Pastor Burns. He introduced himself, and the women, obviously upset, said they were the aunt and sister of Rodney Park.

Burns knew right away something must be wrong. Rodney and Janice were members of his congregation at Cathedral of Faith in Chowchilla.

He asked them to sit down, and they, in turn, told the small group what little they knew of the kidnapping.

No one said anything for a few minutes. Who would kidnap a school bus? Bertie flicked on the radio next to her and tried to find the news.

It was the Dairyland School bus, she had heard the two women say. Many of those kids asleep out there in the cabins had been in summer school, Bertie was thinking. She wondered now at her own insistence that some of them come up to the week-long camp. She had called several parents to coax them. Kammie Mason was here, her mother had finally agreed to let her miss the last week of summer school.

Bill Parker had refused. She wondered if his daughter, Barbara, had been on the ill-fated bus.

She had also called Rodney Park.

The news came on and everyone listened intently.

"Still no word on the mysterious disappearance early today of at least eighteen school children and the bus driver who were kidnapped from a Dairyland School bus . . . among the missing are Lisa Barletta, Mike Marshall, Irene, Stella, Linda and Julia Carrejo. . . ."

Bertie stopped short. "Oh, Lord, not Mike, not Kandi's brother," she prayed. She thought of Kandi Marshall and the close relationship they had developed during the last few days, the hikes they had taken, the talks they'd had.

Kandi had never been to church before and was practically dragged up to the camp by her friend, Bev Polston. They had stayed up talking about it the entire night before Bev was to leave for camp. Bev told her she would meet a lot of boys at the camp, but that's not why Kandi decided to go. She couldn't bear to be separated from Bev.

Bertie tried to bring her attention back to the group around her. More and more it seemed like she was dreaming. The rest of the world seemed so far below them, high up on the mountaintop.

The women rose to leave and the pastor and the counselors gathered around them for prayer. They joined hands, standing in front of the fire in a circle and asked God to bring the children home safely.

Then, out they went into the stormy night, with promises to return if they heard any news.

Bertie was still thinking about Kandi. How was she going to tell her about the kidnapping? She started walking towards the thirteen-year-old's cabin and thoughts of the recent week flooded her mind.

Although Kandi had never attended church, Tuesday night during the camp church service, she had walked forward and accepted Jesus as her Savior.

It was an exciting time for her and the next two days had been spent in long talks to answer Kandi's many questions. And to calm her many fears, Bertie recalled.

She could still hear Kandi praying for God to take away her fear. And now her brother Mike was gone. Kidnapped. Maybe dead. How would her young faith stand up to this? Bertie worried.

When she got to the cabin, she could hear talking inside. One look at Kandi told her she already knew. One of the other girls had been playing a radio when the news bulletin came on.

Kandi was staring at the wall, not responding to any of the girls. They told Bertie she was in a trance. But Kandi was thinking about Mike and how understanding he had been lately towards her. She wondered if her father knew yet and how her mother was doing. She prayed silently for Mike.

Finally she spoke to Bertie.

"Mike is in God's hands," she said quietly. "It's up to God what happens to him."

Bertie left the cabin, her heart and mind full of prayer. These last few days had clearly been a preparation for Kandi, for this trial she was facing.

God allowed her to experience fear earlier, Bertie decided, so we could help her. She thought of all the discussions and the Scriptures they had studied together dealing with fear.

Now that this had happened, the groundwork was already laid. Bertie prayed for Mike's safe return.

But she prayed more for Kandi to be strong.

CHAPTER FOUR

Madera County Sheriff Edward "Ed" B. Bates had a lot on his mind.

Now that the bus had been found—empty—he had plenty of work ahead of him. Temporary command headquarters were set up at the Chowchilla police station and within hours, on-duty and off-duty personnel from other law enforcement agencies had gathered.

California Highway Patrolmen, officers of the Merced County Department of Fish and Game, Tom Walsh of the FBI's Merced office and several detectives from the Madera Sheriff's Department gathered in the crowded back room of the police station.

So many things needed to be done. And quickly. Bates was making assignments: retrace the bus route, interview students who got off the bus, search the surrounding countryside on foot, talk to parents for descriptions of the children and what they were wearing.

The weather was fast becoming a tempest. A storm this time of year in the central valley was so unusual. More than one person had remarked it was kind of spooky.

But despite thunder and lightning and pouring-down rain, a house-to-house search would be necessary.

Volunteers came forward. The sparsely dotted countryside surrounding Chowchilla contains many abandoned barns and ranches, remnants of once active farms. Any one of those places could hide some two dozen kids and maybe a couple of vans. They would all have to be checked.

The Identification Bureau had found tracks near the bus that appeared to be from vans, Bates was thinking, and several residents had reported seeing suspicious vans in the area the last few days.

One, a 1971 Dodge, painted white, was suspicious enough that a woman had copied down the license number and phoned it in to a Chowchilla policeman. Now, he remembered the call and ran the license number through the Department of Motor Vehicles. It turned up a phony registration and an all-points bulletin went out for the Dodge and possibly two other vans.

Nancy Tripp, one of the last children to get off the bus, recalled seeing a white van traveling north on Road 16 after Ed Ray had dropped her off.

It wasn't much, but it tied in.

Another difficulty facing the sheriff was contacting the parents. There were too many to keep calling by phone and they weren't sure yet of just who was on the bus. They had to wait until the parents called in for information, then ask them to come in to describe the children and what they were wearing.

Possible motives were being discussed. Sheriff Bates and Police Chief Gary Brown considered it might be a kidnapping for ransom, but Chowchilla is not a wealthy community. The average family income is only around $9,000 annually.

Brown knew, however, that Ray's wife, Odessa, and his sister, Esther Danieli, worked at the Chowchilla Bank of America. Both women knew the combination to the vault.

That puzzled Brown, though, because there was never more than $50,000 in the vault at any time.

More likely, it was some political terrorist group. That prospect was even scarier.

Jammed phone lines were becoming a problem. The police switchboard had only four lines and they were busy constantly. Brown was worried the kidnappers might not be able to get through.

Pacific Telephone started working immediately to bring in extra cables and provide more lines.

In the tiny wood-frame home on Alameda Avenue, forty members of the Carrejo family crowded into the living room to say the rosary for their four missing sisters. There are eleven children in the family, several grown up and away from home. This night, they brought their own families back home to comfort their mother.

"Hail Mary, full of grace, the Lord is with thee. Blessed art thou amongst women and blessed is the fruit of thy womb, Jesus. Holy Mary, Mother of God, pray for us sinners, now and at the hour of our death. Amen."

Over and over, the Carrejos prayed that Irene, Linda, Julia and Stella would be brought home safely.

Outside of her prayers, Celia Carrejo found it difficult to talk about her children's disappearance without crying. Her eyes avoided the walls where pictures of her four youngest girls were a painful reminder of happier days.

She could almost hear her daughter, Irene, at the piano and could practically feel them dancing on the floor to their favorite music.

"All I ask you, is let me be there. . . ."

Their lives had been filled with music for so long. Irene was such a talented musician already. With scarcely a lesson she taught herself to play the piano, guitar, clarinet, flute and saxophone. All the girls sang and danced. And how Julia loved the Mexican dancing.

She snapped back to reality.

Now, the piano stood silent.

It was eleven o'clock Thursday night before Jim

and Leanna Estabrook had an explanation for Johnny's disappearance. It was raining and thundering. The lights in their Truman Street home went out. They sat huddled together on the couch trying to figure it all out. Jim tried to keep his composure, conscious of Leanna's advanced pregnancy, but he broke down repeatedly.

Together, they prayed out loud, asking God why this was happening to them, but they couldn't shake the feeling something awful was about to occur.

It's as if the wrath of God has come down upon the world—and upon our son, Jim thought that night. He walked outside and pleaded, "Please God! I'll give my own life in place of those children. Please. Give us some sign they're okay." The storm only got worse.

The Gonzales' home faces a narrow alley called Defender Street. Socorro Gonzales prayed continually in Spanish for God to bring her boys, Roberto, eleven, and Andres, eight, home safely.

Her uncle, Jose Redagado, shared the burden and the long hours of prayer and waiting.

His faith was strong. "It is in God's hands if they live or die. He is the only one who can help them. He knows where they are. We pray for Him to keep them safe.

"Not the FBI or the police know where they are. Nobody knows. But God knows."

Evelyn Reynolds started praying as soon as she realized her children, nine-year-old Becky and thirteen-year-old Judy, had disappeared.

A friend, Sheila Armstrong, came up from nearby Fresno to pray with her.

No one slept at the Reynolds home Thursday night and, by dawn, the family doctor was called to give Evelyn a sedative because she was unable to calm down. She was emotionally exhausted from crying. In her mind, her faith was unshaken, but her heart cried out in pain. Still, she never questioned God.

"You have to have enough faith to believe. But you can't question what God is going to do. It is just a nightmare."

Gloria Daniels was convinced the disappearance of her daughter, Darla, was not God's doing.

"I know God doesn't punish," she prayed, "but if we ever did anything wrong, please forgive us and bring our little girl back.' "

Like many other parents, Joan Brown felt sure the storm Thursday night was an indication that God was furious. She never wavered in her belief that her children, Jeffrey and Jennifer, were safe and coming home.

Although she didn't feel close enough to God to pray herself, she went to someone whose faith she trusted.

"I called my close friend, Pat Handly. She's been searching for answers and she's been closer to God recently than I have. I asked her to say a prayer and she said she would call others, too."

About that time, Connie Fletcher called from Hayward with a strange message:

"You know, I'm not really religious—and I'm not even sure He's really up there—but I have some friends here at work who have already started a chain of prayers. And I asked them to do it!"

Judy Hinesley is a devout Catholic. She prayed constantly for her blonde, seven-year-old daughter, Sherry. It was difficult to tell when one prayer left off and the next began. She almost panicked at the onset, but as soon as she had time to think and pray, a calming peace soothed her.

"I can't go off the deep end. I really can't get too shaken up about it. I just know she is okay. And no matter what is happening, I know God is taking care of her. He always has."

Judy explained her confidence to her husband, Tom.

"The Lord has always taken special care of her.

I don't know why, but He does. When she was born, my first husband and I were already separated. He left when I was two months pregnant.

"She could have been born deformed because I went hungry for two to three months. There were so many times when He took care of her. I started fooling around with drugs when she was five months old. I was by myself and He still took care of Sherry.

"He made sure that no matter what I was doing, she was okay. And she came out of it all smelling like a rose. She has no emotional scars at all from the past.

"I know she's okay . . . she's always been His special person."

Sam Barletta could barely talk about the disappearance of his daughter, Lisa, without crying.

He and his wife, Matilda, were still carrying the emotional scars of the death of her twenty-year-old son, Dale, on Christmas Day just six months earlier.

And now Lisa.

Could they take another hurt like that?

About four o'clock Friday morning, President Ford asked the FBI to enter the case. Fifty-five agents came from San Francisco, Sacramento,

Los Angeles and Washington, D.C. They began arriving within five hours of the president's order, along with media people from all over the country.

While law enforcement officers—many volunteering their time—tramped through mud in the stormy night, calls continued to flood the Chowchilla police station.

Many were cranks, several claimed to be psychics. None could provide any real information.

By morning, so many leads had come in, law enforcement units all over the state were employed to check them out.

Because of his excellent reputation, and the parents' expression of confidence in him, bus driver Ed Ray was soon eliminated as a suspect.

At daybreak, planes were in the air. The California Highway Patrol sent their traffic surveillance planes up, while farmers who owned planes in the area and National Guard pilots searched the foothills in their aircraft.

Finally, they got a break. A call came in from the former police chief of a nearby town. He had received a call from a woman who wanted to stay anonymous. She had observed a white van and a dark-colored van parked fifteen miles from Chowchilla off Highway 152. She had seen the vans Wednesday and Thursday and thought they were suspicious.

She took down the license number: 1C91414. The van was last seen about one-thirty Thursday afternoon leaving Los Banos heading toward

Chowchilla (a forty-five minute drive from there).

The FBI had set up headquarters in Bates' Madera office, with one phone a direct line to Washington, D.C.

Bates hand-delivered his new information about the vans in Los Banos to the FBI.

CHAPTER FIVE

After twenty-three years of bus driving and a lifetime in Chowchilla, Ed Ray knew the entire vicinity like the back of his hand.

He was relying on that experience and his exceptional sense of direction as the vans sped along the crisscrossed country roads. Making mental notes of left turns and right turns, he strained to guess their destination. Vivid mental pictures of the countryside he had scoured since his childhood overflowed in his mind.

Despite his mental mapping, it wasn't long before he was completely confused and forced his mind to stop trying to figure it out. What difference would it make anyway—he might never live to tell about it. He turned his efforts to calming the children. He and they were sweltering from the heat.

Irene Carrejo, the oldest girl on the van, scooted over to Edward and whispered softly so the little children couldn't hear.

"Edward?" she said, her voice hesitant. "Is this some kind of joke?"

Edward knew he had to be honest. "No, honey. It's not."

Irene tried to hide her tears so the younger children wouldn't be afraid. Two of her younger sisters, Stella and Julia, clung to her for security. But she couldn't get her third sister, Linda, off her mind. She was in the other van. Irene prayed she was still alive.

Jennifer Brown was getting angry.

"If we're not home by five minutes past the time the bus is supposed to be there, my dad will have the cops out after you," she shouted at the kidnappers. The drivers of the van were separated from the passengers by a thick board, so they couldn't hear her threats.

"Shut up!" Irene warned. "Be quiet or you'll make them mad."

The vans started to slow down and eventually stopped. The children and Ray opened their eyes wide and snapped to keen attention. They heard mumbling. They listened intently for any clue but it was impossible to make out the words.

"Let me out, I want my mommy," a little girl cried out.

"Please let me out. I have to go to the bathroom," another pleaded.

"Shut up in there," came the harsh response.

Ray shushed the crying, whining children and tried to be firm. "Be quiet now, kids, we don't want to make them mad."

Everyone strained to figure out what was happening outside. Some heard metal scraping against metal. Then liquid spilling.

Mike, in the white van, felt his nose burn and sniffed. Gas fumes. The sickening vapor slowly filled the van until all the children could smell it. Some were coughing. The abductors must be refueling.

The vans started up and rolled on again.

Their stomachs told them it was about dinner time.

"I bet my mom's having dinner right now," Mike thought to himself. "She will never believe I got kidnapped. She'll probably be mad 'cause I didn't do my chores."

Mike was brought back to reality by the children, who once again were plaguing him with questions.

The whining and crying disturbed him, never having been around little kids much, but he answered their questions the best he could. There was little room for him to stretch out his legs, so he wound up lying down. The littler children laid on top of him.

Mike tried to keep his mind a blank because

every time he thought about what might come next, terrifying possibilities flashed through his mind.

They were going to die. It was a strange feeling for Mike. Funny how it seems these things always happen to someone else—never to you. And now, terrible as it was, it was going to happen to him.

The possibility never totally left him. He repeatedly pleaded to God using the only prayer he knew. It was the one his mother had taught him.

"Our Father, who art in heaven. . . ."

To keep his mind off their uncertain fate, Mike tried to see where they were going by peering through a screw hole.

The muffled roar of the engine lulled some of the children to sleep.

Irene Carrejo and Lisa Barletta tried to calm those who still were restless in the green van. Weakly, they began singing a chorus of "Boogie Fever."

"She's got the boogie fever . . . Boogie down . . . She's got the boogie fever . . . It's really goin' around now. . . ."

The children begged and pleaded with their captors to stop so they could go to the bathroom. The only answer they received was the low drone of the engine going on and on, endlessly.

Finally, in desperation and humiliation, they were forced to go in their pants. One little girl couldn't wait any longer. Stella Carrejo was lying beneath her and the urine ran down into her face.

"You peed on me!" Stella gasped in disgust. "Gosh darn it. What did you do that for?"

Jennifer Brown handed Stella her shirt to wipe off her face.

The other children finally had to go in their pants as well.

The putrid smell of urine, sweat and the gasoline made them gag. It only grew worse as the children cried hysterically for their mothers and fathers and begged the captors to tell them what was happening.

"Where are you taking us?" they pleaded. "What do you want with us? Please let us go!"

Jennifer sang a verse of "Get Down Tonight."

The other children listened, but their eyes were on Ray. Time after time, they turned to Ray for answers to their questions.

"Why are they doing this to us?" they cried, unable to understand why Ray, an adult, didn't know all the answers. They mercilessly pulled at him for any inner strength they might gain

But Ray could barely hide his own fear.

His mind kept returning to his wife, Odessa, and his sister, Esther, who both worked at the Bank of America and knew the combination to the safe there. Would they be forced to produce a ransom to save the lives of the children and himself? Would they be killed whether the ransom was paid or not?

The brakes screeched to a halt again. Metal against metal. Oh no. Gasoline again and that awful smell. It was all they could do to keep from vomiting.

The van began to sway back and forth and Ray felt his stomach shift. The mountains. They must be in the foothills, he decided. No telling what the men would do with them. Maybe leave them in the forest to die.

The vans halted again. Ray heard brush scraping the undercarriage. The blower had stopped and in a very few moments, the oxygen supply was severely dissipated. Suffocation. They all were suffocating. Ray desperately tore off a piece of the carpet and paneling which lined the wheel well. He put his nose next to it and breathed a frantic gulp of air.

The children who were still awake listened. They heard noises of a canvas material, perhaps a tarp, being pulled over them. Then silence.

It was difficult to be certain how long they were parked. Everyone dozed off from time to time trying to get some rest for their eyes, which were dry and burning, partly from their tears of fear and anguish and partly from straining to see in the darkness of the van.

Sleep came as a peaceful, if temporary, escape from the terror of being out of the secure, protective reach of their parents. They assented to it with sighs of exhaustion. The storm didn't disturb their slumber. They had driven into the mountains and none of the children even remember hearing the thunder which rocked Chowchilla that night in the valley below.

Irene Carrejo and Jennifer Brown couldn't sleep.

They sat up and talked nervously during those hours about whatever popped into their minds. They looked over and periodically checked a sleeping child or shook one awake from a nightmare.

Suddenly, they stopped talking. Their eyes widened, looking into each other's.

They heard the cab doors open, then slam shut. The engine started. They were on the road again. Jennifer imagined the way they would die: they would be lined up against a building and shot.

It was about three-thirty in the morning when the vans rumbled onto a gravely, pitted road. The children were awakened suddenly and they were thrown against each other as the vans jostled up the path.

Finally, the vans came to a halt.

"Bus driver?" one of the men commanded. "Where are you?"

"I'm right here, by the doors," Ray answered. The double rear doors to the van opened wide. The children gasped hungrily for fresh air.

"Out here," he ordered.

Ray rose up protectively.

Relieved that they didn't take one of the children and terrified about what they had planned for him, Ray crawled out.

The doors closed.

The children strained their ears to hear . . . a shot . . . a scream . . . a cry for help. But there was only silence.

What are they doing to Edward? they wondered. The suspense tormented them. Are they killing him? Are they beating him up? Are they going to kill us?

CHAPTER SIX

Odessa Ray watched the sun rise Friday morning.

It cast a golden glow over the thirty-three acres of cotton and corn she and Edward had farmed for thirty-four years, ever since he brought her there as his bride.

She could almost see his strong and husky, five-foot, seven-inch, 175-pound frame loading hay, as always.

The very thought of it made her close her eyes to shut out the painful image.

She hadn't slept that night. Her eyes were closed only in prayer. She didn't dare shut them for fear she would see the terrifying images of what might be happening to Ed and the children.

Odessa felt the power of the prayers of those

around her strengthen her own, but there was no tempering her dread certainty that she never would see her husband again.

Ed could never be considered the tall, dark and sophisticated type. Nor is he brilliant or educated, but his gift of common sense makes him wise. He is a simple, earthy, honest man, and a teaser in a very charming way.

Odessa looked around their home with tears in her eyes. It was totally remodeled from the time she and Ed had first moved there. There is lovely, velvet furniture in the living room and comfortable early American in the family room. She thought about the hours she and Ed had worked together to get these things they wanted. Ed always had been a good provider. He had worked two or three jobs for years. His days started early in the morning and many times they didn't end until long after dark.

But then, he had always worked hard. One of seven children, Edward was born in Le Grande, just nine miles from Chowchilla. Five of his sisters and brothers still live within two miles of him.

He attended Dairyland School as a young boy when his parents first moved to the ranch in Chowchilla. Even then he worked hard to help make a living out of the land. He went on to Chowchilla High School when he finished at Dairyland. He was no honor student, but he did exceptionally well in his industrial arts classes. He also played varsity baseball and basketball his first two years of high school. His junior year, a new coach was hired who insisted his players be at every practice. That ended Ed's career in sports—he had to milk 130 cows every day. There was no way he could do that and make every practice.

Odessa and Ed had grown up in Chowchilla and knew each other for years as friends, but their romance did not blossom until Ed was twenty-one and driving a milk truck for his father. Odessa rode on many a milk route with him just so they could be together. They were married June 30, 1942, six months after their first date.

Odessa glanced over at the television set, where the pictures of their grandchildren were proudly displayed. It hadn't been so many years ago that the pictures there had been of their two sons, Glen and Danny, who were out searching now, fear and determination aging their young faces.

Through the night and early morning hours, they searched relentlessly. If only Ed could see how much they cared.

Lights were burning in many of the homes in Chowchilla that night. Dawn gradually washed away the shroud of shock protecting the hearts of the children's families. Their minds cried out for understanding.

Why would anyone want to take their children? They had no money, no influence. Why Chowchilla and not a wealthier area like Beverly Hills? Why this bus load of children? What could they want from them?

The impact of the possible answers made them wish the questions had never occurred to them.

News reports reminded them that the "Zodiac killer," still at large and claiming responsibility for murdering thirty-seven people in the Bay Area, once had said he thought a bus load of school children would be appropriate victims.

"School children are nice targets," he had said. "I think I'll wipe out a school bus some morning."

Could the followers of Symbionese Liberation Army (SLA) members Bill and Emily Harris have planned the abduction to insure a trade for their leaders then on trial in Los Angeles? The parents could only shudder as they recalled the bizarre details of Patty Hearst's kidnapping two years before.

Could the motive be ransom? Did the kidnappers know that Ed Ray's wife and sister were privy to the combination to the safe at the bank?

Could it be followers of convicted mass murderer Charles Manson? Newspapers reported that he once bragged that he would kidnap a bus load of children and raise them according to his beliefs.

And, in whispers, some wondered if it could be a flying saucer. What else could swoop down and steal the children without a trace?

One of the strangest speculations was a story brought to the attention of the police by an anonymous woman caller, a published short story remarkably similar to the kidnapping of the children. Police, FBI and sheriff's investigators pored over "The Day the Children Vanished" by Hugh Pentecost.

The story tells of the disappearance of nine children, who were on their way home from school in a station wagon converted into a bus.

Coincidentally, the action takes place in a small mining town and, as in Chowchilla, there is no trace of who or what has taken the children, who disappeared as if an interplanetary vacuum cleaner had sucked them up. The bus in the story vanishes on a regular run along a two-mile stretch of road bordered by a lake on one side and a mountain wall on the other. Absolutely no turnoff could explain its disappearance. The book's bus driver, like Ed Ray, is a model of respectability and reliability and engaged to an employee at the local bank.

In Pentecost's tale, the station wagon is commandeered by four gunmen, driven inside a moving van and taken to a nearby barn where the children are hidden.

Some of the children's clothing, in the mystery, is found floating in a deep, water-filled quarry, which sends the parents into a panic because they fear the children are at the bottom.

The secret to the story is uncovered by the bus driver's father, who decides the clues they are finding are illusory. He believes the kidnapping is a fake and the clothing in the quarry a trick to get the people out of town so the criminals can rob the bank. Following his hunch, he surprises the would-be robbers at the bank.

The children are returned safely.

Could the kidnappers have gotten their idea from this story? Were the police being distracted so they could commit amother crime somewhere else? How far would they take it? If only the parents could depend on the same happy ending.

But that, they feared, was too optimistic even to hope for.

More passionate than the debates over motives were the demands for revenge.

Jim Estabrook could not get through to the police station by telephone. The lines were jammed. So he drove downtown to hear the latest news. There, he was cornered by a reporter from one of the television networks, who asked him what he thought should be done with the kidnappers.

"At first, all I wanted was my son back," answered Estabrook. "But now I'm starting to get mad. I want something done to these men."

"Just what do you have in mind?"

"Well, if you were a parent in the same position, I think you'd know."

Estabrook immediately regretted his statement. His comments went right on the air and were picked up by other stations.

Oh, my God, if the kidnappers hear that, they might do something to my son, Estabrook thought. Why did I have to go shooting my mouth off?

The interview played every ten minutes on the television network and Estabrook spent the afternoon in fear that this remark could cost him his son's life.

Chowchilla is a farming community of forty-five hundred people in the heart of the San Joaquin Valley. Its fields are heavy with grapes, cotton, sugar beets, almonds, alfalfa, tomatoes and corn. Most of the men there own firearms for hunting.

Said one farmer, "If those kidnappers come back, they'd better be careful. People around here have guns and know how to use them. I know if I saw one of those boys and I had my gun handy, I'd rightly blow his damned head off."

Vigilante groups brandishing shotguns and pistols combed the area searching for any clue. All day, they patrolled the surrounding almond and fruit orchards.

"If they catch the people who did this, there'll be some hanging," Jerry Delaney, a plant worker, predicted ominously.

Meanwhile, Sheriff Ed Bates, with his army of FBI agents, California Highway Patrolmen, sheriff's deputies and posse members, was coordinating the most extensive manhunt of his career.

Thrust into the midst of national attention, Bates was becoming something of a celebrity.

A colorful character known for being outspoken, Bates had gained national notice a year before in a dispute with the Madera County Board of Supervisors over the cost of operating patrol cars. He ceased all patrol functions after the board refused to transfer $23,000 into his budget for gasoline. It worked. Patrolling was resumed four days later when he was assured he would have the money.

Even before that, not long after he took office, Bates had warned the board that he would ask the attorney general to send in troops to patrol the county if more money was not allocated to his department. He got his money.

Completely bald, Bates is a familiar figure in his western hat. He is an avid talker, especially when it comes to law enforcement. A co-worker says he has seen Bates make an off-the-cuff speech on law enforcement it would have taken others days to prepare.

And now, once again, the heat was on. But Bates was cool, working day and night on the investigation.

"He eats it up," commented Undersheriff James Haney.

President Gerald R. Ford sent word to the parents that he was "quite concerned" for the safety of the children and the bus driver.

Ford's press secretary, Ron Nessen, said the president asked the FBI to supply a written report and to keep him personally informed on a less formal basis as well.

The FBI announced that it had actively entered the investigation and assistant director Robert E. Gebhardt of the Los Angeles office was directed to take personal charge of the investigation.

The ordinarily still morning hours were alive with the crackle of radio static as citizen's band radio operators organized search parties on foot, in jeeps and on the freeways. Painstakingly, they combed the barren acres surrounding the tiny farm town.

The unmistakable rasp of breaking channels interrupted conversations throughout the day.

"Station members are taking off from work," a voice informed John Moody, head of CB base operations. "We have jeep, horseback and foot help. I know where I can get more foot help tonight. My wife set a deal up. They've gotta have someplace to eat and get something to drink . . . Blue Streak out. . . ."

Moody had his CB radio operation set up on a table in the parking lot of the Chowchilla police station.

Dorothy Champ strained to speak over the radio interference.

"We were taking our boys for a ride when we heard the announcement about the kids over the radio," Mrs. Champ said, sipping soda pop in a camper nearby.

Her eyes were bright and excited despite the thirty-three hours she had sat in the camper without sleep.

"We were all ready to go to the coast with the children and we circled to turn around and come over here to see if we could help."

They helped set up base operations in the parking lot to coordinate CB search efforts statewide.

A breaking channel interrupted her conversation. Moody had more instructions for another search party.

Moody is a building contractor. He took the day off to aid in the search. His wife, Tina, came along too.

Dorothy eagerly passed notes to police as the CB-ers assisting in the search turned up possible clues. The Champs stayed up all night so expert rifle team members called in on the case could sleep in their camper.

"I think the police are pleased with us," Tina said, pride coming through her voice. "They are working with us. They have asked us not to say anything around the parents, because they might overhear and get upset . . . So we pass the word on with notes and don't say anything."

She looked toward a police car. "Is that officer Riley? Officer Riley, you are supposed to use the back entrance."

Tina looked tired but her eyes suddenly brightened. "I think people realize now CB is not a toy."

Norman Hodges, a Fresno County reserve

sheriff's sergeant assigned to assist with CB-police communications, said law enforcement officials appreciate the CB-ers' capabilities.

"We figure there are ten thousand truckers with their eyes peeled."

The CB efforts constantly were monitored by the confused parents, who refused to budge from their stations near the radios.

Reporters from major national and some international newspapers, plus network television crews, began filtering into the city to cover what was fast becoming the hottest news story in months.

By midday, more than 250 journalists had flocked to Chowchilla to cover the story. Fire trucks were moved out of the fire station on Trinity Avenue to make room for all the camera equipment, lights and microphones.

Pacific Telephone had installed extra cables and brought in dozens of special news phones and banks of pay telephones to meet the need. The phones were in use constantly and reporters lined up to use them, pumping coins into them as if they were hot slot machines.

The reporter would put a dime in the slot, dial the operator, get a busy signal, then reach for the dime in the coin return slot. The cycle would be repeated several times before reaching the operator to get a line out.

The town's two motels were booked by noon Friday, forcing many to go to Madera or Merced for lodging. A number of journalists from outside the area flew to Fresno where they rented recreational vehicles, drove to Chowchilla and used them as their command posts.

Thea Wilson, New York *Daily News* correspondent, could not get an airplane flight from Los Angeles and hired a taxi to drive her for $200.

"It would have been cheap at twice the price," she commented.

There was little room for typewriters; reporters set up portables on car hoods, in the backs of vans or on their laps, trying to get a story out.

Townspeople gave food to the hungry journalists and the Salvation Army set up a canteen to serve refreshments.

The firemen and the Chowchilla police, under Chief Gary Brown, showed unusual patience in handling the media crush, offering assistance and cooperation.

The heavyweights of the journalistic world were on hand to report the largest kidnapping in the history of the nation.

Besides correspondents from *Newsweek*, *The Washington Post*, *The Baltimore Sun*, *The New York Times*, Reuters, the British Broadcasting Corporation, *The Chicago Tribune* and the Springer Foreign News Service of West Germany, a number of state and federal officials made appearances.

Although most of the media personnel stayed close to the fire station waiting for official word, some ventured out to try to talk to the families. They approached the families apologetically, sorry for interrupting them and intruding on their lives at this private, painful time.

The Bill Parker, John Brown III and Bob Reynolds families kept themselves available to the press at all times, grateful for the help it was providing in the search. They were also eager to thank the parents across the country for their support and prayers.

Some allowed the reporters into their world of torment, but others slammed the doors in their faces.

The Heffington family, secluded in their darkened farmhouse on Avenue 23½, did not come to the door. A friend answered and stepped outside. He wore sunglasses to hide the emotion and strain of the day.

"The family will see no reporters. And don't take any pictures—even of the house," he said forcefully. "The family is upset by you even being here."

The reporters apologized and left.

CHAPTER SEVEN

Just down the street from the chaos of the Chowchilla police station, Margie Parker sat in the quiet of her living room.

She stared at the boxes stacked next to her chair, seeing them, but not seeing them. How important they were to her just a few days ago. She had wanted to get a head start on the move into the family's new home. It would be finished next month. But now, it just didn't matter. Nothing did. All that mattered was Barbara, her baby, the youngest of her six children.

She wandered through the house in a fog, trying to avoid the bedroom down the hall, where Barbara's favorite teddy bear lay alone on the bed.

No matter how her friends and family tried to comfort her, she couldn't shake a haunting feeling of guilt that somehow she might have prevented what happened.

"Somebody was trying to tell me, 'Don't send her,'" she told a friend with certainty, her voice breaking with emotion. She was sure the strange morning of Barbara's disappearance was a warning.

Everything went wrong that day. One of Barbara's sisters had to stay home because she was vomiting. When Margie went to the refrigerator to make Barbara's sack lunch for summer school, there was nothing for sandwiches. The confusion of everyone getting ready for school and work and tending to a sick child was only worsened when Margie had to ask her husband, Bill, to go to the store for lunch fixings.

"I wanted to send her off with a good lunch," she lamented, her voice betraying a futile effort to contain her tears. "I should never have let her go. I feel terrible about it."

Margie was not the only one regretting her actions.

Pam Barletta, thirteen, clung to her father, Sam, as they searched the bamboo thicket where the bus was found and her sister, Lisa, had disappeared.

The young girl's churning emotions exploded into hysterics and guilt.

How could she forgive herself for insisting Lisa go to school when she, herself, didn't want to go?

Her parents tried to comfort her by reassuring her it was not her fault. But still, there was that awful feeling. Over and over the early morning scene replayed itself in her mind, tormenting her.

"Lisa! Get up! It's fifteen 'til seven." Still half asleep, Pam turned and went back to bed. She was just dozing off when she realized her sister still wasn't stirring. If Lisa didn't go to school, Pam would have to go and pick up her own art projects. She really didn't want to go. Her mother needed her at home.

She tried again. "Lisa, get out of bed, it's seven-fifteen. You're going to miss the bus."

The girls' mother, Frances Williams, heard the exchange between the sisters and sympathized with Lisa.

"Leave her alone, Pam, let her sleep," she instructed.

But Pam was insistent and gave it one last try. She went in the bedroom and threw her sister out of bed and onto the floor.

"Okay! Okay!" Lisa growled. "I'm up!"

Convinced that her sister was sufficiently conscious, Pam reminded her to bring her artwork home from school.

Mission accomplished, she went back to bed.

Lisa hurried to catch the bus.

Jim Estabrook left home at 7 A.M., before his son, Johnny, was even out of bed. His morning at Trailmobile-Pullman Company, where he worked, left him shaken the rest of the day, hardly prepared for what happened later.

He had walked around the plant about eleven that morning when he noticed a man pulling a big, 440-volt wire through a conduit. He walked over to help, when suddenly the electricity short-circuited, jumping from the wire down the pliers in the man's hand to a pipe lying near Jim's feet.

"I was only a few feet from him when it happened and he was thrown right past me. We both flew about twenty feet. It was just lucky he had rubber handles on those pliers," Jim said, shuddering.

"We both should have been dead," he concluded in amazement.

The incident kept him jumpy all day. "After that, I felt like everything else would go wrong too. The whole day was weird," he remembered thinking. "There was just a feeling in the air."

As Joan Brown waited for word on her children, a number of isolated incidents slowly became related. Was she being warned?

At about the same time the bus was being hijacked, Joan was looking out her window at the Chowchilla Insurance Agency where she works part-time.

Something was wrong, she sensed. It was nothing she could put her finger on. Perhaps it was the storm brewing in the sky, strange for this time of year. There was just an odd, eerie feeling in the air.

Her children were unusually affectionate toward her that morning. In retrospect, it seemed as if they knew what was coming. But of course, they couldn't have.

Jeffrey, ten, had portrayed Samuel Adams in a school play and he had made a special point to come down into the audience to tell her how glad he was she was there.

Then, as she was leaving the school, Jennifer, nine, ran over and gave her a kiss, turned to walk away, then ran back and gave her another one. She started to walk away again and returned a third time to kiss her. It wasn't like Jennifer at all.

Shirley South, a postal employe in Chowchilla, could only thank God over and over for her two girls, who came home safely from summer school that day.

Both her daughters were close to one or another of the kidnapped children. Michelle Brock had begged Barbara Parker to come home with her on another bus.

"I don't know why, mama," Michelle later explained to her mother. "I just felt I should do that. For some reason, I really wanted her to come home with me."

"That was so unusual," Shirley related, shaking her head in disbelief. "The girls never have asked to bring kids home with them."

Shirley was convinced the Lord used her daughter to give Barbara a second chance.

"The Lord often works through people to get

them to do things," she said. "It was so funny the way it happened. It was as if the Lord picked and chose the ones he wanted to get off."

Molly Brock, six, was even closer to the incident. She boarded Ed Ray's bus by mistake at the swimming pool, but was able to correct her error when he stopped back at the school to pick up more children.

Marlene Smith kept her two daughters off the school bus for the first time in the six-week summer school session.

She said her nine-year-old daughter, Cindy, felt ill, so she decided to keep her and her other daughter, Charla, seven, home too.

The children had ridden the bus home from school every day before Thursday.

"I don't know why I decided to keep them home," she reflected.

If Mrs. Woody James had even stopped for gas on her way to pick up her children, Debbie and Michael Eye, their names would have been on the list of missing children.

Mrs. James decided at the last minute to pick her children up from school and arrived just as the children were boarding Ed Ray's bus.

Dorsmae and Fred Hansen's seven-year-old son, Von, was yet another spared.

His regular bus ride home was on Dairyland Bus

Number One. A playmate, Richard Moore, had been begging Von to come home with him to play after school. For three days prior to the kidnapping, Dorsmae had said no to their requests because she had no way to pick up her son in the evening. However, on that Thursday morning, she received a telephone call from the little boy's mother, saying, "Please, can't Von come and play for a while?"

"No," Dorsmae insisted once more, "I'm sorry, but I just don't have a car to pick him up later."

"Oh, that's no problem, I'll bring him home," Mrs. Moore promised. Dorsmae agreed. Her son escaped.

This was the second time in four months one of the Hansen children had brushed disaster. A daughter, Laurie, was coming home from college with three other students when their Volkswagen bus spun out of control and rolled over four times. Laurie had traded places with one of the other students so he could have more leg room just minutes before the accident occurred. The young man who sat in her place was thrown out of the automobile and killed instantly. Laurie received the fewest injuries.

The very morning of the accident, a letter came addressed to Laurie describing a need for missionaries in Australia.

"We knew she was spared because God had work for her to do," Dorsmae related. Laurie left for Australia within two weeks of the day her brother escaped the kidnapping.

"Naturally, any parent feels grateful when her child is saved from something like this," Dorsmae reflected. "But I certainly don't feel holier-than-thou. It could just as easily have been Laurie on that seat in the van.

"You can't help but identify with the other parents. You feel hurt for them, fear for them. You hate to see someone else go through something like that. I like to think the Lord takes care of His own, but those other children are His own, too. We are just very, very thankful."

Seven-year-old Sandy Zylstra was the last child to be dropped off the bus before her summer schoolmates vanished.

Another of the Zylstra daughters, Eveline, nine, had to be taken home from school at eleven when she started vomiting.

Their parents, Ted and Tine Zylstra, give all the credit to God.

"The Lord is faithful to those who are faithful to the Lord," said Tine. She and her husband attend church at the Cathedral of Faith every Sunday and take their girls and five-year-old Jerry along with them.

"I am so hurt for the woman—Mrs. Carrejo—who has four daughters on that bus. My prayers are for all the families, but especially for her."

The good fortune of her daughter being the last one off the bus has spurred many to exclaim, "Somebody from above was sure watching over you!"

CHAPTER EIGHT

Ed Ray stared intently at the masked men who now faced him.

The four of them were enclosed in a canvas tent. In one corner was a hole in the ground. Ray didn't dare speculate what that was for.

Besides, he wanted to memorize those faces. He wanted to be sure he would never forget the men responsible for this nightmare.

"What's your name?" the captor snapped.

"Ed Ray."

"How old are you?"

"Fifty-five."

"Take off your pants," he demanded, raising his gun.

Ray loosened his belt uncertainly. Then he unsnapped, unzipped and slipped the trousers over his new boots. He stood in his underwear as he handed over the trousers.

"Now, the boots."

Again, Ray complied.

Too frightened to feel embarrassed, Ray walked toward the hole. One of the men handed him a flashlight and two sets of batteries, then a book of matches. He put the matches in his shirt pocket. They motioned for him to climb down a ladder. He winced as he cut his hand on some ragged wire.

He looked around and immediately recognized his prison as an old truck body shell with the wire mesh lining exposed.

The children were now alone in the darkness, without even Ray for security. The little ones burst into tears.

The abductors turned to their young victims.

The doors of the green van again were opened wide. The captors ordered a child out and closed the doors.

Jodie Heffington and Jennifer Brown were arguing.

"I want to be the last one out," Jennifer insisted.

But Jodie was afraid for her friend. She was sure the abductors would kill the first, middle and last child off the van.

"No, you're not," insisted Jennifer. "I'm going to be last."

The doors opened again. Another child was taken.

Like slow torture, the children imagined their

horrible fate as they waited for their time to come.

One by one, the children in the green van were led along the tarpaulin-lined path.

Each child, like Edward, was asked for his or her name, age, and was forced to hand over an article of clothing or a piece of jewelry.

The children in the white van had been building up identical fears of this new place.

"They're gonna kill us. They're gonna kill us," cried eleven-year-old Robert Gonzales.

The double doors opened. The men pulled out the first child. The doors closed.

"I volunteer to be last," Jeff Brown announced, scooting to the rear of the van.

The doors opened again.

Jody Matheny crawled out.

Again they closed.

Jody walked obediently down the path.

"Name?"

"Jody Matheny."

"Age?"

"Ten."

They looked him over.

"Hand over your glasses," the man demanded. Jody reluctantly removed them. The world instantly became a dark blue for Jody, who is legally blind and has a progressive eye disease. The condition worsens when he is forced to see without his glasses.

Anger was welling up within the youngster. What'd they have to take his glasses for anyway? Weren't gonna be any good to anybody else.

"And your shoes."

That did it. Jody had had enough. He jerked his brand new tennis shoes off and threw them at the captor. One shoe was aimed at the man's face, but he raised his arm just in time to block off the shoe. The canvas sneaker bounced off his arm and struck Jody in the forehead.

Jody was shuffled into the three foot wide hole lined with wire mesh and climbed down a ladder into the underground prison.

When it was Mike Marshall's turn to climb out of the van, he took a deep breath and crawled across the carpeted floor. He was weak with suspicion, exhaustion and lack of oxygen from being in the hot, confined van for so many hours.

He felt his legs trembling beneath him as his boots touched the ground.

"Name?" a gruff voice demanded.

"Mike Marshall."

"Age?"

"Fourteen."

"Empty your pockets."

Mike pulled out a book of matches and six cents.

"Your hat, kid."

Mike reluctantly removed his cap.

This cap had special significance to the Marshall family. Mike's mother bought it in Reno, where her husband was riding in a rodeo. She lost money in the slot machines and when Bob also lost at the rodeo, she decided it had not brought her the luck she had hoped for. She gave it to Mike when she got home.

Now, it was in the hands of the abductors. They showed him the way to the hole.

Each child went through the same routine.
"It's okay. Everything is going to be all right," Ray assured each one as he helped them down the ladder.

The ladder was pulled up when the last child was entombed. The men threw down a roll of toilet paper.

"How long do we have to be here?" Ray called out. "What are you going to do with us?"

"Twenty-four, maybe forty-eight hours," came the reply.

Suddenly, the whole magnitude of what was happening to them crashed in on him.

He begged and pleaded.

"Please, please let the children go! I have grandchildren—I want to see them again!"

His cries were answered by a huge iron plate, which was being lowered to seal the entrance.

The children had shyly avoided looking at their friend, Edward. They were embarrassed for him as he stood in his undershorts and socks. It made them hate the kidnappers all the more.

Their eyes and ears strained as they floundered in the darkness. Ray used the flashlight to examine the inside of what they believed would be their mass grave.

It appeared to be the shell of an old semi-trailer, about twenty-five feet long, eight feet high and covered with wire mesh.

In one corner was a supply of corn flakes, Cheerios, Honeycomb, potato chips, bread, peanut butter, twelve five gallon kegs of water and two makeshift toilets. Fourteen mattresses covered the floor.

Two ventilation pipes with fans were built into either end of the top of the van. There were two candles on a ledge of the wall.

Their nightmare had only begun. The youngsters screamed in terror as they heard the sound of dirt being shoveled over the entrance and the sound of wires being cut. They became aware of the ceiling, which was bent ominously downward.

Would the whole ceiling cave in on them, burying them instantly in a mass grave?

Shrieks filled the black pit with a penetrating fright that reached even to Ray, who pleaded once more with the merciless hijackers, "Please, mister! Let us out! I have a blank check! I'll pay you! We'll do anything! Please, let us out!"

Jeff Brown didn't think that was such a good idea.

"No way," he decided. "If we have to do anything, I'm staying in here. They could tell us to go rob a bank or anything."

Judy Reynolds was discouraged and crying.

"Oh, God," she cried out. "Why is this happening to us out of all the people in the whole, wide world?"

The children were exhausted and hungry from the long ride.

The younger children grabbed for the boxes of cereal and loaves of bread. Like starving little animals, they stuffed themselves. The dry cereal was a feast and the water cool and refreshing as they quenched their parched throats.

Mike Marshall watched the little ones gorging themselves, but he carefully took only a little. Mike was thinking ahead. Later on, they might need it more.

Jeff Brown's thoughts were running along the same lines. He watched his little sister, Jennifer, wipe out the first box of Honeycomb. But he couldn't bring himself to eat anything.

"Who knows how long we'll be here?" he thought to himself. "I don't know how long this food will last. We might need it later. I could stand to lose some weight, anyway."

Jodie Heffington encouraged Jeff to eat a little something, but he stubbornly refused. Finally, concerned for his welfare, she stuffed a handful of Cheerios and a bite of peanut butter sandwich into his mouth.

Irene Carrejo and Lisa Barletta, both twelve, were two of the oldest girls captured. Irene is one of eleven children and three of her younger sisters were in the van as well. Lisa has an older sister, Pam. Lisa and Irene assumed the primary responsibilities of becoming substitute mothers to the younger children.

Jody Matheny, a gentle boy, also understood the younger children's fear. Though he was handicapped far beyond the others because of his faltering eyesight, he was stronger than most. Overcoming his own uncertainty, he held them in his arms and reassured them everything was going to be just fine. He would take care of them.

Before the older children considered tending to their own growling stomachs, they checked the cereal and bread supply and made sure the younger ones' tummies were full. Once the children were fed, the girls held, rocked and sang to the youngsters until they seemed comforted.

Michelle Robison, eleven, was particularly concerned about Monica Ardery, who at the tender age of five was the youngest child on the bus.

"I want my mommy," Monica cried in an unceasing flow of tears. Michelle held her and soothed her.

Before long, Michelle became the mother Monica couldn't survive without.

"Mommy, mommy," Monica whispered softly to her as she drifted off to sleep.

In the early morning hours it was cool in the hole and the children wrapped up in the blankets, huddling together to keep warm.

Their stomachs were finally full after hours without food and their little bodies were warm. Many fell asleep.

Meanwhile, under the stress of their shared ordeal, all the normal youthful dislike for the opposite sex melted away.

Mike had his arm around Judy Reynolds. Ray looked over at them. He was mildly alarmed but decided not to say anything.

"This may be the last huggin' up he ever does," Ray thought sadly.

Jody tenderly cuddled Sherry Hinesley and one of the Carrejo sisters in his arms.

Relishing his role as protector and comforter, Jody looked into the blur of their faces. Confidently, he told them, "Calm down now. Everything's going to be all right."

Everything *was* going to be all right, Jeffrey thought. "Come on everybody, let's pray!"

"To who?" queried a voice from a dark corner.

"To anybody that'll listen," he joked. "I'm praying to God and Jesus."

There was no room to get on his knees without stepping on someone, so Jeff sat alone and prayed. At first, he was afraid God might not listen to him because he didn't go to church regularly.

He started making promises.

"If you'll get us out of here," Jeff prayed, "I'll go to church whenever I can and I'll . . . I'll . . ." The words came hard. So did the promise.

"I'll stop cussing," he breathed in a rush.

Nearby, Jennifer was making her own promises to the Lord.

"If you let me out of here, I'll go to church every Sunday. I'll be good and I'll clean up my room and I'll always feed my fish," she promised.

Jeff's faith was strong. He tried to help those who were weaker. He encouraged others to pray.

Jody couldn't concentrate enough to pray, but he had a peaceful feeling in his heart. And in his mind, he knew Jesus was watching over him and would help him get out.

"Edward! What time is it?" someone asked for the hundredth time.

Becky Reynolds was singing a song she'd learned in church, "This Little Light of Mine." No one else knew it, though, so she returned to her prayers. She asked God to help them and kept her favorite Scripture verse in her heart:

> For God so loved the world, that he gave his only begotten Son, that whosoever believeth in him should not perish, but have everlasting life.
>
> —John 3:16

Her sister, Judy, was praying too. As she did, she made a new commitment to God: for the first time, she put her trust in Him.

Sherry Hinesley broke away from her usual prayers of "Hail Mary" and "Our Father" and began to speak from her heart in spontaneous prayer.

To help keep their spirits high, Jeff ran through all the jokes he knew. He took off his shirt and lent it to Becky Reynolds, who was wearing only her bathing suit. He was still wearing two pairs of trousers from the stage play in which he'd participated at school Thursday.

He offered the extra pants to Ray, but they were too small. One of the little girls put them on.

Jennifer watched her brother make the offer to Ray and stifled a giggle as she looked at his funny, hairy legs.

The children were delighted to have toilets to use, but there was no privacy.

Irene Carrejo and Jennifer Brown were the first girls to face the problem. They devised a buddy system where one held up a blanket while the other used the bare wooden hole that was their toilet.

Jeff Brown didn't bother with the blanket.

It's dark, he thought. What the heck? No one's gonna laugh at me now.

Some of the exhausted children fell asleep. Some sat alone in silent prayer. Others started singing songs.

"If you're happy, clap your hands," someone began.

No one clapped.

"If you're sad, cry . . ." she continued.

"Booo-hooo," the children eagerly contributed.

Jennifer nursed hurt feelings as she watched her big brother helping several of the other girls. His girl friend, Linda Carrejo, was demanding all his attention and Jennifer was getting none. Then, Monica Ardery crawled into his lap, put her arms around his neck and called him Uncle Jeff.

When Mike woke up from a short nap, he lay on the mattress looking around the van. Maybe they could get out of here. His eyes scanned the four walls. There had to be a way.

It had been twelve hours since the twenty-seven victims had been lowered into this cramped hell.

Ray became concerned about the ventilation.

The air was already smothering, hot and muggy, making breathing a chore. Twenty-seven people in twenty-five feet of van. The fans probably were hooked up to the car heaters up under the tent above them, Ray decided. When those batteries went dead, they were dead.

His stomach turned as he envisioned twenty-six children suffocating. What if the men never intended to come back at all?

Ed Ray does not take personal responsibility lightly. If they were to survive this, it would be on his shoulders. If they didn't, that, too, was his responsibility.

But was an escape even possible? Should he risk the kids' lives trying to get out? Those men could have killed them at any point all along the way. If they were going to kill them, wouldn't they have done it by now? The kidnappers probably were still in that tent above them standing guard. Would they open fire on them if they tried to escape? Ray couldn't be certain what was waiting for them up above. But he was certain that death was waiting for them if they stayed where they were.

They would have to try.

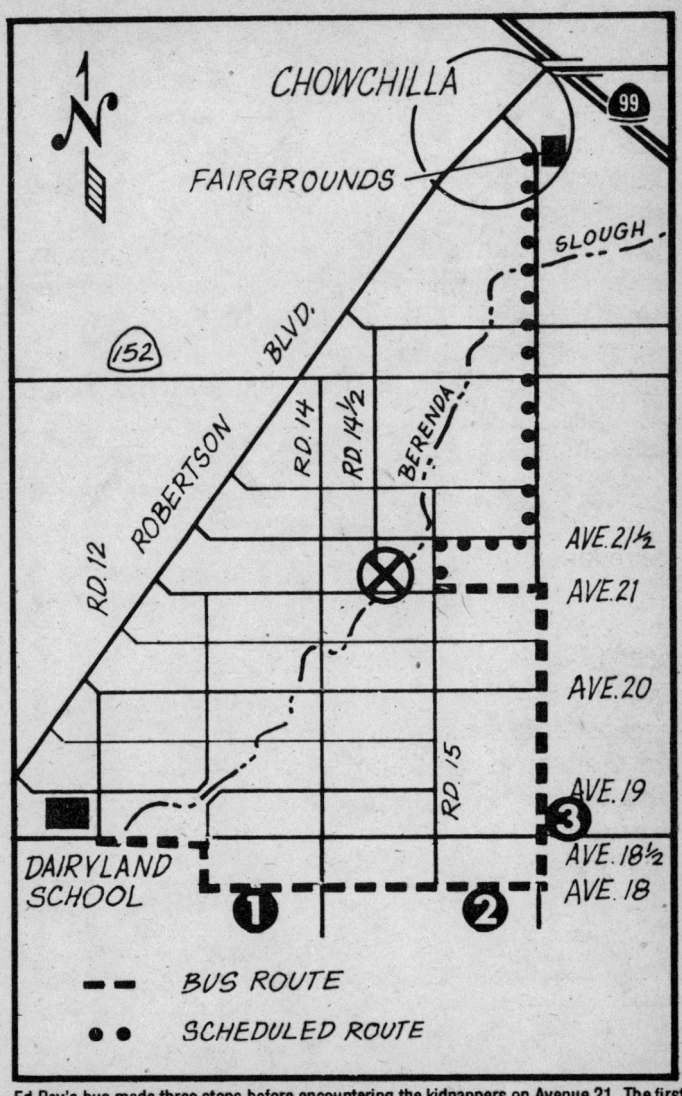

Ed Ray's bus made three stops before encountering the kidnappers on Avenue 21. The first stop was to drop off Edward Gregorio, the second was for the three Tripp children. Number 3 shows where Sandy Zylstra got off. X marks the spot where the empty bus was discovered. (Map by Richard Nakaguchi of the *Fresno Bee*.)

The modest school building from which the bus departed. (Wide World Photos.)

The abandoned bus as Sergeant William Cooley found it about seven-thirty on Thursday, July 15th. (Ralph Thronebery, *Fresno Bee*.)

The rock quarry in Livermoore, California, where the abductors buried the truck van in which they concealed Ray and the children on Friday. The circle surrounds the exact location of the van.

This photograph of the inside of the van was taken after authorities excavated the van and opened its doors for viewing. Photographers were not allowed inside. (Wide World Photos.)

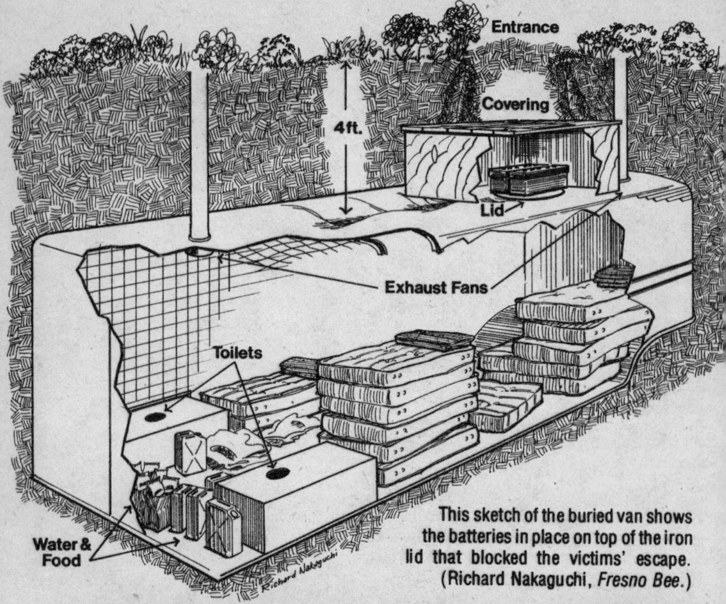

This sketch of the buried van shows the batteries in place on top of the iron lid that blocked the victims' escape. (Richard Nakaguchi, *Fresno Bee*.)

Ed Ray faces his first press conference with his wife, Odessa, at his arm, Saturday morning, July 17, at about four-thirty. (Ralph Thronebery, *Fresno Bee*.)

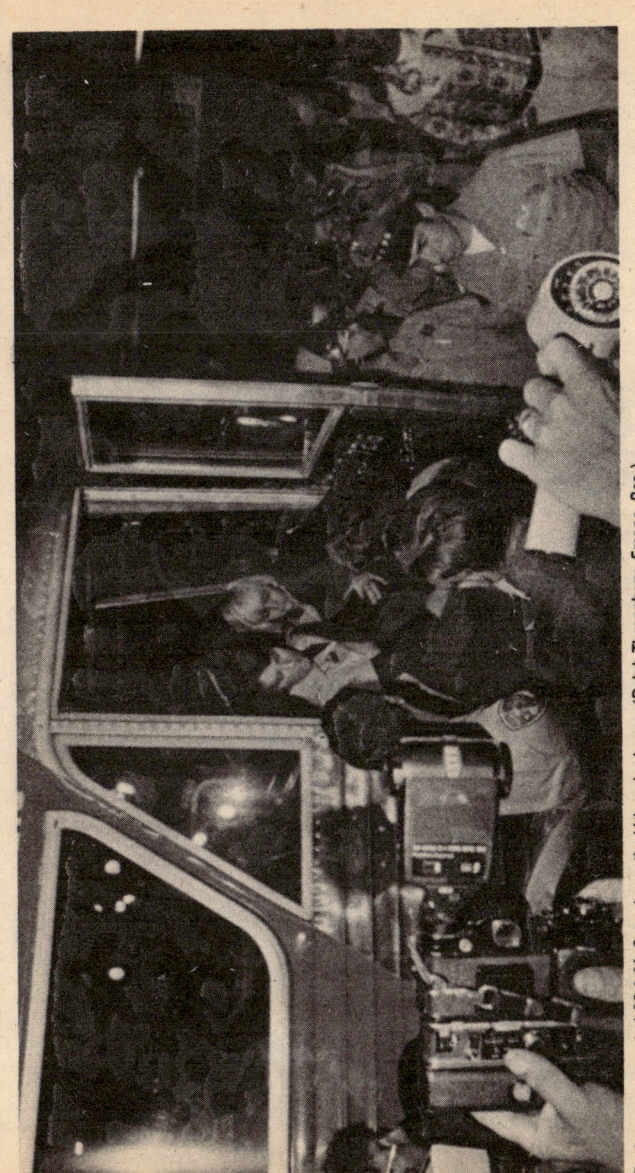

The joyous moment, 4:00 A.M. Saturday— the kids arrive home. (Ralph Thronebery, *Fresno Bee*.)

Lisa Barletta's mother, Frances Williams, left, had just learned her daughter was safe when a photographer snapped this shot of her embracing her friend, Barbara Kjostad, in the Chowchilla Fire Department. (Wide World Photos.)

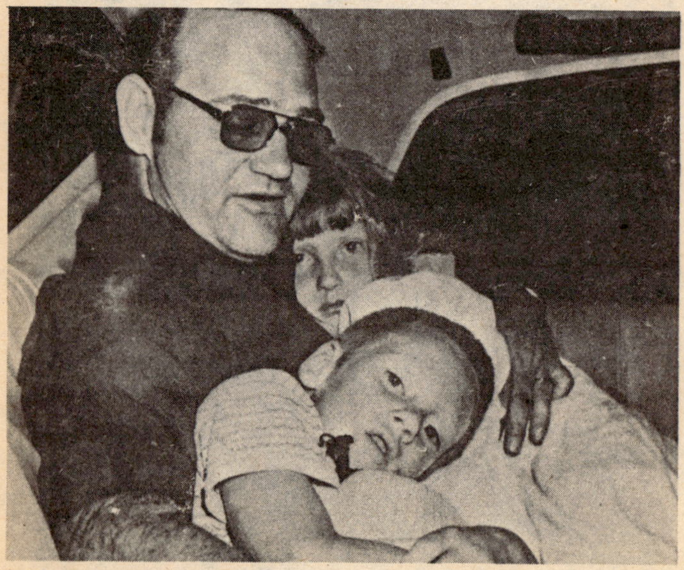

Rodney Park cuddles his two children, Andrea, eight, and Larry, eleven, after their early morning reunion. (Wide World Photos.)

CHAPTER NINE

It were better for him that a millstone were hanged about his neck, and he cast into the sea, than that he should offend one of these little ones. —Luke 17:2

The Rev. R. S. Van Buskirk looked up from his Bible and into the faces of the solemn congregation which had gathered in the First Baptist Church to pray for the kidnapped children and their bus driver.

He looked into their eyes: many were crying, others were closed in their own silent prayers. Some wore dark glasses to hide red eyes. He added his own, even stronger, statement to that of Jesus which he had just read in the Gospel of St. Luke.

"Perhaps it were better for such an individual

never to have been born," he whispered.

"My God, why?" asked Van Buskirk, sharing his distress when he heard the news the children were missing. "Why these little ones? Why these children?"

The Rev. John Surratt, pastor of the First Assembly of God, stepped up to the pulpit.

"Prayer is the power that will loosen the bondage on the children," he said. He told of a similar crisis in his own life when his brother was kidnapped in Texas and taken sixty miles from his home. All the while, their mother prayed for her son's release.

His brother was released unharmed. Dramatically, a couple abducted by the same kidnappers was murdered.

"My brother was spared because of prayer," Surratt affirmed emotionally.

He encouraged the congregation to pray that the Holy Spirit would remove any anger, revenge or vindictiveness from their hearts.

"Instead," he said, "have love for them [the abductors] as God had love for us when we sinned."

The people filed quietly out of the service. They put their arms around each other. They touched the hands of weeping friends next to them, shared their fears and praised God for the work He surely was doing to protect the children.

One woman took off her dark glasses as she stepped outside the church. Her eyes were tired and red. "I feel empty," she shared. "You think you're safe living in a small town. You never think anything like this would happen here.

"Those things only happen in the big cities. We thought we were so lucky to be here."

Another woman said, "I didn't know any of the kids. I just came to pray."

Van Buskirk thanked God that none of his parishioners were among the missing.

Some were scheduled to ride that bus, but they were off together on a camping trip.

There were no parents of victims at the prayer vigil. They chose to cling together at home: reflecting, speculating, praying.

Pat Robison was certain that God was protecting her two daughters, Angela, nine, and Michelle, eleven. She and her husband, Mike, prayed many times that afternoon in their small farmhouse on Avenue 22½.

"When they couldn't find them with the police or the FBI, I knew God was the only one who could help," she said.

But despite her faith, she couldn't help envisioning her family of four girls being drastically changed overnight to only two.

Could God be so cruel as to take away two of her children? she cried.

The young parents wondered how their daughters would take their captivity. The lightning would frighten them, they knew that for sure. Angela would probably be all right, they thought, but Michelle would scream in terror.

Janice and Rodney Park wrestled with a memory. It was only a few years ago that Rodney's brother, Richard, had accidentally backed over his own two-year-old daughter in the driveway.

Richard had become very protective of his niece Andrea after that.

"No one will ever hurt Andrea as long as I am alive," he had promised himself and he shared the promise with his brother and sister-in-law.

Now, Andrea and Larry might both be dead. He felt so helpless. Who were these men and how could they dare take these children right out from under them?

The incident was on everyone's mind. God had taken one child in the family. Would he take two more?

Rodney couldn't live with the pain. All he could do was cry uncontrollably. The doctor prescribed tranquilizers and Rodney spent the rest of the day groggy, slipping in and out of a deep, protective sleep.

He woke up just long enough to see if there was any news. And to whisper to God, "Please don't take mine. Please don't take mine."

Janice continued to cling to the Scripture her sister had given her earlier that morning. Romans 8:28 echoed time and again in her mind: "And we know that all things work together for good to them that love God, to them who are the called according to his purpose."

Another friend reminded her, "There's no way anything can happen to those kids. They belong to the Lord. He gave them to you and you gave them back when they were dedicated. There's just no way God is going to let anything happen."

The Parks are active in the Cathedral of Faith, an Assembly of God church in Chowchilla.

"Rodney and I have never disbelieved, but we have been a little lukewarm at times," Janice admitted. "We don't always take the time to go to church because Rodney works shift work at a food processing plant. His schedule is a week on days, then a week on nights."

The Parks were reasonably certain that Andrea would be able to handle the situation all right, but they worried about Larry, a hyperactive child who, without medication, runs nonstop twenty-four hours a day. Before the doctor prescribed those pills, his mother had to lock him in his bedroom at night to get any rest because he slept very little. What would these circumstances do to his already abnormal brain waves? Would it all explode into an emotional collapse?

They could only place him in the Lord's hands.

Andrea would be fine. Janice was certain of it. The Lord had always taken extraordinary pains to see to it that Andrea was provided for.

Janice had had many problems getting pregnant. When she finally conceived, she and Rodney decided to see a group of obstetrical specialists in Fresno.

She would lose this baby, the doctors explained. After that happens, come back to Fresno, they said, and we will correct your problems so you can carry a baby full term.

Surprisingly, Janice didn't lose the baby. With the exception of a kidney infection which had her in bed for a week, Janice enjoyed a storybook pregnancy.

When a crisis began in labor, Rodney's mother immediately began a prayer chain. As she approached fifty hours of hard labor, the elder Mrs. Park told friends, "There's something wrong with that baby. I know it. I've got to get to the hospital.

"If anything happens, that child [Rodney] will lose his mind."

The delivery finally came, however, and Janice gave birth to a healthy baby girl, Andrea. Afterward, the doctor quietly called Rodney aside.

"I cannot take credit for delivering this baby," he confided. "I was the attending physician, but a power greater than I delivered your child.

"We never let a woman suffer like that," he told Rodney, "and I don't know why we did this time. But if we hadn't, and we had punctured the placenta ourselves, the baby would have died. There was only one place where the placenta could have broken safely. Anywhere else, your baby would have bled to death."

Bennie and Jean Campbell didn't wait in the police station where some of the other parents gathered.

"I can't stand to listen to them," she declared. "I

don't like what they are saying. They think the kids are dead, that they will never see them again. I can't listen to that."

The Campbells had more to worry about with their son, Jody Matheny, than most of the parents. His eye condition had left him partially blind since birth. She glanced over at the Braille homework he brought home just last week. It was to prepare him for the day when his sight would be completely gone.

Would the kidnappers have taken away his glasses? she wondered. If he was in bright sunlight, it could cause his eyes to be damaged even further.

She and her husband prayed off and on during the afternoon. A friend called from Concord to let them know her whole church was praying for Jody's safe return along with the other children.

Jean Campbell really didn't know what to think but she tried to keep her mind on God. He is in control, she thought over and over to herself. He is with Jody. Lord, help me through this.

Darla Daniels also has health problems which were of much concern to her mother, Gloria. "We just moved here in January from Eureka for Darla's health. She has rheumatoid arthritis and asthma. We were hoping the heat here would burn it out of her system."

Certainly the dampness from the rain would not be helping.

The Estabrooks have lived in Chowchilla two years, but eight-year-old Johnny has only lived with his father since spring. His mother had custody of him prior to that, since his parents had divorced several years ago.

"Just when I was getting used to having him around," Jim cried out. "Why did this have to happen to us?"

Waiting in the small living room of their apartment with the television never off for a moment and the carpet wearing thin from his pacing, Jim scratched his head in bewilderment.

" I still can't figure out why it's happening here. You move to a small town to get away from the kooks and the weirdos, then they come down here in our little town and take our kids away.

"Why? Will you tell me that?" There was no answer to his question and it hung in the air for a moment. Then a bulletin came on the television screen and he jumped to his feet to turn up the sound.

". . . still no clues in the search for the missing . . . ."

He switched the set off in anger.

"When are they going to find out something? All we keep hearing is speculation, that maybe it's the

Zodiac killer or the SLA or stuff like that. I just can't stand it...." His voice broke again and he left the room.

"He's beside himself," his wife, Leanna, said. "He can hardly keep himself together." Her red and swollen eyes reflected his pain. She switched the television back on to see if anything was happening. Her seven-month pregnancy making her weary, she decided to rest.

Spirits were high at the Brown farmhouse and neither John nor Joan were worried or fearful. It was an uncommon feeling for Joan, who is usually a pessimist. Inwardly, she continued talking to her children, Jeffrey and Jennifer, over and over again, reassuring them they would be all right. She believed they were comforted.

John thought the kidnappers wanted to trade the children and Ed Ray for Patty Hearst, the Harrises or Charles Manson. He, too, felt the children were safe.

"The neighbors think we're kooky," they said. They were grateful to their friends for being with them, but thought they were too morbid. Someone had brought tranquilizers for Joan, certain she would be hysterical in her anguish. She wasn't, but one girl broke down twice while visiting at the Browns'. She was given the tranquilizers.

One thing the Browns were certain of, the country should learn a lesson from the kidnapping experience. "I don't want all this to die down and just be forgotten," Joan reflected. "This can bring about a definite change in law enforcement, with stricter penalties and more protection for the victim.

"If people will just realize that overnight, their kids can be snatched from them, they'd spend some time with them right now.

"Values have to be taught to a kid. Can you imagine any child given love and taught respect for others, doing something like this? I can't."

As they talk, the Browns smoke one cigarette after another, their only sign of nervousness. The day of the kidnapping, John, who had kicked the habit in February, started smoking again to ease his tension.

Through the window one can see twenty acres of permanent pasture, Jeffrey's pigs and Jennifer's horse and pony.

John used to be a Chowchilla policeman; now he teaches welding at the high school.

Their children will handle themselves differently when they return, the Browns believe. Jeffrey is a sensitive lad. His mother reports that when he would see things on television that upset him, she, in turn, would say, "That's why we live out here. Things like that don't happen here.

"He'll never believe me again," Joan said, sadly.

"Jennifer is a little mother and is probably taking care of the little ones," she surmised.

"One thing puzzles me," John wondered. "As

many farmers as there are around at that time of day, why didn't someone hear them?"

Joan was quiet. "I think they must be sedated."

Later that afternoon, while washing her hair in the first moment to herself since the ordeal began, deeper thoughts began to whirl about her mind.

I know I'm not in shock, she was thinking, because I'm functioning normally. Maybe I should make a deal with God. Is there something I've got to promise? But I can't promise. I'm not strong enough to follow through with it.

God is really trying to get hold of me and I'm not getting the message. Yes I do believe in God, she consoled herself, but this other—accepting His Son as her Savior—no, I just couldn't.

I'm still fighting . . . how much longer am I going to fight? she wondered. The possibility stayed in her thoughts, yet still she could not do it.

She had been raised in the Methodist church and left because of disagreement with certain political views, specifically, the church's involvement with Cesar Chavez and Eldridge Cleaver. Later, she tried the Baptist church, but found too much hellfire and damnation to suit her.

My God is not a vengeful God who is going to strike you dead if you don't do this or that, she thought. She was baptized twice but felt it didn't "take" either time. It meant a lot to her at the time and, at other times, when things got rough, she did return to God, which only made her feel guilty.

She had been fighting a long time and still pride wouldn't let her surrender her will. Even now, she was still fighting—even when her children's lives were at stake.

Margie Parker prayed continually to herself.

"I have so much fear," she related. "I am thinking the worst. I am so afraid of what condition Barbara is in. I pray to God He will give her the strength to stand whatever it is she has to go through.

"I don't know what kind of people have her or what they want to do with her. If she has just one person to comfort her, she'll be okay. And there are a lot of children old enough . . . my hopes are higher today," her voice trailed off.

Bill Parker saw more sense in keeping tabs with the police and the FBI, than in prayer.

"I believe there's a God, but I think things like this are out of His jurisdiction. I'm not praying. It just depends on what you believe.

"I believe in the police department, the FBI and the press. We never see God in action. Suppose a bus jumped off the freeway and all the kids were killed. If the parents had known it ahead of time and prayed, would it have made any difference? If an accident's going to happen, it's going to happen. I'm not an atheist, but I believe if you live your life like you're supposed to, you'll be okay.

"I'm a realist. I just hope whoever these people are, they will take care of the children."

Like many of the fathers facing one or more

missing children, there was the added responsibility of emotionally distraught wives and families.

"We fathers—I've talked with several of the others—are very concerned about our wives," Bill said. "Of course, we're very concerned about the children. But we also want to keep things together at home, as heads of our households."

Much of the praying in the Parker house was done by fourteen-year-old Sharon, who prays diligently every night. Her faith that God would bring her sister back never wavered.

On Avenue 23½, Tommy Van Hoff waited for word about his seven-year-old daughter, Cindy. He chain-smoked as he talked with his family and friends.

"There are times when the littlest things bother her and other times, nothing bothers her. It's hard to say how she'll do."

His thoughts raced over all the possibilities: where could the children be?

His wife, Linda, was praying. A Mennonite minister lives across the street and he and his wife came over to comfort the Van Hoffs.

"I was praying for God to bring Cindy home," Linda recalled. "But I didn't try to make any bargains with Him. I knew I couldn't keep my end of the bargain so I didn't make any deals.

"But I'm hoping He'll keep His end of the bargain."

Tom and Judy Hinesley found it impossible to sit at home. They dashed from the police station to a CB radio to a police radio. They even went looking for clues on their own.

"The Lord is really working through the CBers," Judy was convinced. "Can you imagine what those kidnappers think when they hear that thousands of truckers are out to get them?"

A prayer was constantly on Judy's lips, but Tom found it a little more difficult.

"He is worried and very upset," Judy explained. "I think he is more worried than I am. But his faith isn't quite as strong. He doesn't have enough faith right now to fall back on. He is living off mine.

"We never pray together. We're not ready for that. But, if there's something he really wants, he brings it to me to pray for."

Sherry's nighttime bed partner, sister Kristina, three, was trying to put the pieces together in her own simple way.

Over and over, she repeated, "We gotta find Sherry. The bus took Sherry. They gotta bring her home."

Mrs. Donald Ardery never left the police radio in a friend's truck as she waited for word about her two daughters, Lisa, and little Monica, the youngest child on the bus.

"I think both girls are strong," she said firmly.

"I think they can handle it." Her voice was tired, but she added with tearful pride, "The FBI men told me I've got beautiful girls after they saw their pictures."

Judy and Becky Reynolds share a room in the small home on South 13th Street. The house looks much like others around it and their room like the rooms of children their ages. Judy turned thirteen in June and Becky is nine.

On the wall is a Ronald McDonald poster. The bed is unmade and toys and clothing are strewn about. No one has gone in there since the girls disappeared Thursday on Dairyland School District Bus Number One.

Evelyn Reynolds was asleep, sedated by her doctor in the back bedroom. Bob Reynolds tried to relax in the brown recliner, positioned in front of the television.

"I'm worried. I can't sleep. Nobody here slept last night. I didn't go to work today—the company told me not to worry about it." Bob's face showed lines of concern that would be permanently etched there.

In the kitchen, his sister, Caroline Gillespie of Fresno, poured cup after cup of hot coffee for family members who sat and waited.

"Everybody's worried. The kids'll be cold and scared. Usually they just wear their wet bathing suits home and put their clothes on over them.

"And last night it was thundering and lightning . . . ."

The Reynolds moved to Chowchilla in November, 1975, when Gray Lift Inc. transferred Bob out of Fresno where he had lived all his life.

The same arguments were heard in homes all over Chowchilla.

"It must have been well planned, well organized," Bob thought aloud. "But why here? Why a small town like this?

"I'll tell you why," he answered himself, "because in the country, nobody expected it. And from Chowchilla, there are three directions they could have taken—north or south on Highway 99 or west on 152. Those are both main roads.

"One thing gives me hope. The kids were so quiet, they must have been nice to them. I feel they're keeping them happy." His voice was reflective.

"And hey! That bus driver is the greatest person in the world. He's like a second dad to those kids . . ." His voice trailed off. There had been some suspicion of Ed Ray at first, but the parents wouldn't hear of it.

Caroline mentioned another heartache the family was experiencing.

"This month marks the tenth anniversary of the death of another son, Ricky. He was only five when he was electrocuted. There was a bare wire inside the cooler," she explained.

It was also in July and had been on everyone's

mind. Until the kidnapping.

"It's unreal. It's a nightmare. I keep waiting to wake up," Bob said.

And down the hall, Evelyn tossed fitfully in her sleep, her body desperately needing rest, her mind unable to be stilled.

Odessa Ray was comforted by Ed's six brothers and sisters who had rushed to her side as soon as they heard the news.

One son, Glen, flew in with his family from Buckeye, Arizona, to share the burden of worry with his mother.

The other son, Danny, searched for his father on horseback with the sheriff's posse.

CHAPTER TEN

But Jesus said, Suffer little children, and forbid them not, to come unto me: for of such is the kingdom of heaven. —Matthew 19:14

Jeff, you are one of the best students I have ever had. Your appreciation for fine literature is a gift from God. He uses us all in a special way. Each day of your life may He use you to help guide and love others.

Beverly Hansen
July 4, 1975

Joan Brown read the inscription in the front of Jeffrey's Bible. Beverly Hansen had been Jeff's teacher at summer school last year. Now she was on hand to comfort and encourage Joan.

"I know the Lord is with Jeff," she reassured. "More than a year ago, He led me to give Jeff that Bible and yesterday, before the kids left on the bus, Jennifer came up to me and said, 'Jeff really likes that Bible you gave him. He reads it every day.' "

Joan could not understand such confidence, but as the teacher unraveled the events of the year before that had led up to the purchase of the Bible, she began to wonder.

"We were talking about discipline and obedience in summer school last year," Beverly said. "I told them how Noah built the ark before the flood. And then I explained why Noah's obedience to God could help the children see why they needed to obey their parents.

"You don't always know why, but you have to do it," she recalls telling her class.

"Jeff came up to me after class and said he really enjoyed the story. Right then, I started thinking about getting him his own Bible.

"My husband, Eric, had just become a Christian and I was saving to buy him a Scofield Reference Bible. One day, I was in the Bank of America and I ran into Pastor Surratt of the First Assembly of God.

"I told him I almost had enough money saved to buy the Bible. He asked me how much I needed and I said about ten dollars. He offered to give it to me out of his own pocket.

"I said, 'No, people are supposed to give the church money.' He persisted. I said no again.

'Give it to somebody who needs it or put it in the collection plate.' "

She smiled.

"If I had taken that money, I'd have bought the Bible for Eric and Jeff wouldn't have gotten his. But since I didn't have enough for Eric and I had just the right amount for Jeff, I bought him a Bible.

"We brought it out here to his house and later, he wrote me the most beautiful letter, thanking me and saying he hoped God would use him."

"I feel the Lord was preparing Jeff in this way. He came closer to God than he had ever been."

Joan Brown let the words sink into her mind. What did they mean? That God had known about the kidnapping ahead of time and still allowed it to happen? That God was using her son in a special way?

What she heard next was even more startling. Beverly continued.

"I talked to a woman—I don't even know her name—in Fresno and she said the night of the kidnapping she and a friend were praying for the kids and she had a vision of a young boy leading the group in song and prayer.

"I just know it's Jeff, I just know it. I feel Jeff will be praying and being obedient to God.

"I have been praying for Jeffrey and Jennifer and I have a real peace about it."

Joan felt the same peace, the same assurance that her children were coming home. Was that faith? If it was, she didn't know she had it.

She recalled Beverly's words repeatedly as she waited and wondered what it all meant.

In nearby Fresno, a young couples' prayer group from Valley Christian Center prayed for Chowchilla, which lay thirty-five miles to the north of them.

"While we were praying, I felt the Lord would have us pray for an anonymous phone tip," Wayne Jacobsen recalled. "It was about eight o'clock Friday."

Another member of Valley Christian Center, Don Warnes, was moved to pray Friday at noon rather than eat lunch.

"I heard the community in prayer in Chowchilla and thought how wonderful it was to see them turn to God for help. I remember praying, 'Lord, open the eyes of the officials so they will see where the men are. Also, Lord, put fear into the hearts of the men who are doing this.'

"While I was praying, I recalled the biblical story [II Kings 7:3-7] of the four lepers who left Jerusalem while it was under seige by the Syrians. They said to one another, why should we sit here until we die? We die if we stay here and we die if we go to the Syrians. They went and discovered that the Syrians had fled, leaving all their treasures behind, because the Lord caused them to be afraid. I hoped the Lord would similarly strike fear in the hearts of those kidnappers."

CHAPTER ELEVEN

Escape . . . Escape . . . Escape. . . .

The idea wouldn't leave Ed Ray's mind.

He examined the predicament objectively. Mike Marshall was the oldest. He was strong. He'd be a big help. Robert Gonzales, too. He was only eleven, but wiry. His family worked a farm and Robert was used to hard work.

He glanced at his watch. It was nearly four o'clock. Not much daylight left.

"Hey, Mike, Robert. Come over here and give me a hand with these mattresses. Let's climb up here and see if we can move that iron plate."

The boys were bored just sitting in the van and were instantly intrigued at the idea of escape.

The mattresses were piled high enough for Ray to stand on top of them and try to budge the plate with his hands and head.

Closing his eyes and clenching his teeth, he pushed.

Nothing moved.

This would never work. That plate was too heavy.

A tool. A punching tool. Something he could jab underneath the iron plate and use for a lever.

He pointed his flashlight to the inside of the hole, searching for something that might work.

He caught a glimpse of a loose piece of wood on the side of the truck body. Climbing down from the mattresses, he stepped over the children and pried the board loose.

He climbed back up and felt around the rim. He looked closer. There was a small niche where the plate didn't quite match up with the hole.

Wiggling, jostling and prying, he worked the wooden board into the opening. He felt the plate give way slightly. By fractions of an inch, he urged the plate sideways. Finally, he had a space big enough for his hand to reach through.

He felt around. Something was on top of the iron plate. No wonder it was so heavy. His neck craned as he reached farther up into the shaft. His mind formed mental pictures of what he was feeling.

Batteries, giant batteries, like in trucks. His despair emerged in a loud groan. Ray's years of working on farm equipment made them familiar items to him. There was no mistaking them.

Those babies were heavy—at least a hundred pounds each. And they had to be moved.

He and Mike worked together for over an hour slowly trying to inch the batteries closer to the edge of the steel plate and slipping the plate farther away from the hole.

Some of the children watched the escape attempt skeptically. They chided the workers sarcastically saying, "You know what's gonna happen when you get up there, don't you? That man will be laughing at you saying, 'Ha! Ha! Ha! Where do you think you're going? Get back into that hole.' "

But they were hoping they were wrong.

When the first battery was close enough to the edge to be pulled in the pit, Ray explained what he was going to do to Mike. He would bring the battery down onto his stomach and Mike could catch the other end and fall with it onto the mattresses to keep the battery acid from spilling onto the children.

Gingerly, the batteries were inched down, then dropped safely on the mattresses. Ray and Mike carried them to the rear of the truck body. But there was little excitement over their progress.

The threat of what was up there waiting for them quelled any excitement their efforts might otherwise have produced.

Ray confided in Mike, "We've got to do this. They may be up there waiting for us, but we're going to kick the bucket down here if we don't."

Mike agreed and with new determination they returned to their task. Mike, too, was strong. The son of a rodeo star, he had already broken into the circuit and was used to the hard work that goes with the glitter of that world.

Once the weight of the batteries was off the iron plate, Ray could move it sideways. He directed his flashlight upward into the shaft, always conscious of the noise he might be making.

All it would take was one suspicious sound from down below and the abductors might be onto them.

The flashlight was dimming fast and he was already on the second set of batteries. If they had to, he figured, they could always use the candles.

It looked like the kidnappers had placed a thick piece of plywood on top of a wooden shaft about four feet deep and three feet wide.

The mattresses weren't high enough to reach up to the top. He would have to climb through the hole made by moving the iron plate and use the plate for a working platform.

He also was going to need a board to chip away at that plywood effectively. He was afraid to take off any more support from the truck shell. Those sides could cave in any minute.

The box springs. He got down from the platform of mattresses and turned one over. Tearing off the covering, he pounded at the wood frame with his board and broke off two nice-sized pieces.

"Mike, we've gotta go up there and move that plywood off the top. It's gonna take two of us."

Mike nodded his willingness to help.

The two climbed up through the hole and crouched on the roof of the truck body. Ray got down on his hands and knees and pushed against the lid with his back trying to lift it up.

Grimacing as he mustered all his strength, he pushed.

It wouldn't budge.

Again, he pushed. Again, it held fast stubbornly.

Again . . . and again . . . and again.

The tension was making him weary by now and sweat was pouring off of him. It had to be more than a hundred degrees in there. Like a human baking oven. Ray could hardly breathe, the stifling air was choking him.

He climbed down to pour water over his face and arms. He was soaking wet before he remembered the matches in his shirt pocket. The flashlight was growing fainter by the minute and now, no matches.

Mike stayed up in the shaft, determinedly poking at a corner with the board. Ray sat down on the mattress to catch his breath for a minute. The kidnappers were still on his mind.

"Dear God," he prayed, "just let us get through this. I don't know if we can make it much longer."

Just as he looked up from his silent prayer for help, Mike managed to wedge his board into the crack between the plywood lid and the sides of the shaft.

Daylight poured in like a million gold coins.

Twenty-seven pairs of thirsty eyes drank in the tiny beam of light, their first sunlight in more than thirty hours.

This was it. There was no turning back now.

Ray climbed back up into the shaft and thought about what to do next. They would have to get the dirt off the top of that plywood before it could be moved. There may be several feet of dirt above them and there was only room for their fingers to dig with.

It was going to take time, there was no question about it.

And the kidnappers. They must have seen the ground move when Mike jammed that piece of wood up there. They must have heard them pounding by now. Ray listened for voices. He heard none. They must be gone or at least they were far enough away that they couldn't hear what was going on.

That was comforting.

But now, there was work to be done. He and Mike continued to pull fingerfuls of dirt down into the shaft. They broke off little sticks from the boards and bit by bit pulled more dirt into the shaft until a pile of dirt built up on the mattresses beneath them.

They worked on both corners where the wood met the shaft, bit by bit expanding that space.

The other boys could see that Mike, Robert and Ray were growing tired. Several of the boys volunteered: Jody Matheny, Jeff Brown, Johnny Estabrook. Ray kept the trickling stream of dirt flowing, trying to get enough room so he could get his hand wrapped around a corner of that plywood to break it off.

What seemed like a hundred times, he groaned

and pulled, but the thick plywood resisted his prodding.

He felt his legs and arms shaking from exhaustion. He couldn't go on another minute. He had to rest.

Weaker than he had ever felt in his life, Ray pulled himself down into the truck. His own perspiration had soaked his clothes and mud was caked all over him. He poured the cool water over himself and collapsed on the mattress.

He closed his eyes for only a few seconds. Suddenly, he felt a resurgence of strength and determination like he had never felt before. Like a robot bent on his mission, he raised up from the mattress and without looking to either side he set his eyes on that piece of plywood. With incredible strength from a source he could not determine, Ray grunted and broke off a hand-sized chunk of the wood.

That was the turning point. They could do anything now.

The digging went much faster after that and within a few minutes enough dirt was pulled down into the van so that they could see outside. Mike Marshall put his eye to the hole.

The tent was gone. The kidnappers probably were, too. They had to work fast. They had gone too far to be thwarted now.

Grabbing the wood with both hands and putting all his weight into it, Ray broke off a larger piece of wood.

It was large enough for a head to poke through.

Mike was closest.

"Mike," Ray said, "now be careful. Take your time and let me know what you see out there."

Ray was afraid of what to expect. Were they out in some godforsaken forest? What would he do in the dark woods with twenty-six little kids? All this would be for nothing if all they had to look forward to was being stranded outside.

Mike saw two old trucks off in the distance.

Ray's fears were relieved and his heart was pounding.

"Do you see anybody?"

"No, sir, nobody."

Ray wanted to scream with excitement but it was too soon to get the kids all stirred up. They had to move fast. Any second the men could be back and their nightmare would begin anew.

He instructed Mike to climb out and brush the dirt off the top of the plywood. That taken care of, Ray could lift the sheet with his shoulders and flip it over onto the ground.

The iron plate went next.

Breathless, Ray climbed back into the van and showed the kids how he, Mike and Robert were going to pass them up to the surface.

Ray's voice was unemotional and matter-of-fact. There was no time for joy, fear, appreciation or excitement. They had to move.

One by one, he passed the little children up to Robert Gonzales who was standing on top of the truck body, who hoisted them in turn to Mike Marshall at the top of the hole.

The children were trying to think ahead.

"Maybe we should take some water or blankets with us," they suggested, already fearing what they may have to cope with next.

But there was no time for that. Ray couldn't risk even one unnecessary second. Getting out of there was all that was important.

"Don't worry about that. We'll all be together, running. You'll warm up pretty fast."

The children were out in minutes. Last of all, Ray grabbed Mike's hand and pulled himself out and up onto the ground.

He could see that they were in some type of rock quarry. There was a light in the distance.

"C'mon kids!" Ray cheered.

As the group ambled toward the quarry, Mike held cautiously back, hiding behind some bushes.

Those workers may have been in on the whole kidnapping plan. He wouldn't be trapped again.

"Where's Mike?" one of the kids asked. Another spotted his hiding place.

"C'mon, Mike. Come on out!"

Reluctantly, Mike caught up with the others.

The filthy little group ran frantically toward the light. Ray could see a man welding and working on some equipment above him.

"Hey," Ray shouted up at him.

The man looked down at this scroungy, dirty character standing in his undershorts and socks, and his own stomach filled with uncertainty.

"I've got a bunch of kids here. We've been kidnapped!"

The man recognized the circumstances instantly.

"I heard about you on the radio at noon while I was eating lunch!"

Ray explained that they had been buried on the quarry grounds.

The welder's eyes grew wide with disbelief.

He signaled another man in a shop on the other side of the quarry and told him to use the phone in there to call the police.

That done, the man from the shop ran over to the kids to see them for himself.

They bought the kids soft drinks and one of the men loaned Ray a pair of his coveralls. Ray borrowed the telephone and tried to call his wife at home in Chowchilla, but the lines into the town were jammed.

Within minutes, a blinding array of sirens and flashing lights barraged the quarry. CB-ers who heard the police dispatch over the radio flocked to the site.

Alameda County Sheriff Tom Houchins and an FBI agent were like bloodhounds within inches of the fox. Before all else, they herded Ray off into a private room to pick his brain for any clue.

Ray looked back at the kids with worry in his eyes. It was cold out there and they still were afraid. He still didn't feel comfortable leaving them alone. They were his responsibility until they were right where they ought to be: at home with their parents.

Houchins assigned two deputies to watch over

the children. "Don't let them out of your sight."

Houchins had to think fast. The kids were hungry, tired, dirty and cold. They had to take them somewhere to be examined by doctors, fed and questioned.

Santa Rita flashed through his mind. There was a prison rehabilitation center nearby. He placed the call and instructed them to get ready to care for a bunch of hungry kids.

Houchins sensed Ray's concern for the children, even now as they were surrounded by police, firemen and FBI agents.

"They are going to be just fine. Right now we need to talk to you."

CHAPTER TWELVE

The Chowchilla Fire Department was a virtual volcano of activity as more than three hundred news reporters and photographers worked to put the sketchy, disjointed information in order.

Families of the kidnapped victims made repeated trips to the sheriff's office, adjacent to the fire station, for news of the investigation.

Teenagers changed their main drag Friday night from Robertson Boulevard to Trinity Avenue so they could watch the national and local news media covering the abduction.

And with all those television lights and cameras, there was more than one attempt by local hams to see themselves on the news by just hanging around the cameramen.

The commotion had reached a steady roar when

a news reporter screamed to the crowd.

"They found the kids and they are *all right!*"

The crowd erupted with an explosion of cheers and screaming. Crying, laughing, jumping and hugging each other, the once-tired people were suddenly rejuvenated. Teenagers driving by began honking their horns. In a mad scramble, reporters raced to get to the phones.

Typewriters clicked like a battalion of machine guns as the news was spread far and wide.

Frances Williams, mother of Lisa Barletta, was in the building when the news was announced. She rushed out of the office, tears streaming down her face. She spotted a friend, Barbara Kjostad, and called out, "They found the kids! They've got Lisa! She's all right!"

They dissolved in each other's arms, crying uncontrollably in relief.

Sheriff Ed Bates had just crawled into bed at the Safari Motel in Chowchilla. He hadn't slept for thirty-eight hours.

The phone rang and Bates rolled over with a groan to answer the call.

"Bates," he answered out of habit.

"They found the kids," came the voice over the phone.

"I'll be right there."

Bates hopped out of bed, dressed in record time, and arrived at the station a few minutes later. Making his way through the reporters, he walked into the office. An officer briefed him quickly: "The kids were found in a rock quarry in Livermore. They're questioning and examining them now at Santa Rita."

"Sheriff Bates, Governor Brown is on the phone," another officer informed him. Bates picked up the phone and the governor asked for verification of a television news report that the children had been found. "I don't know yet, I haven't gotten through to Santa Rita. Hold on a minute." Bates quickly placed a call to Santa Rita, but the officer there would only say he didn't have time to talk, he was busy meeting with the press.

"But what about the kids?"

"They have been found and they all appear to be well."

At the Bill Parker house, the family immediately crowded around the television set to listen to one more special bulletin. This one contained the news they had been waiting to hear. "The twenty-six children and their bus driver kidnapped yesterday afternoon in Chowchilla have been found in a rock quarry in Livermore. All appear to be well." A cheer rang out and by the time the phone call came from police fifteen minutes later, the family already was celebrating.

Neighbor children flocked to the Parker house and Margie could scarcely contain herself. "This is the best birthday, anniversary, Christmas, New Year's—anything present I could ever ask for!"

Sharon and Kathleen, Barbara's two older sisters, immediately slipped away into the bedroom to thank God for saving their sister's life.

Half a mile away on King Street, three-year-old Kristina Hinesley was being cared for by her grandmother, Connie Hinesley. "They found my Sherry! Sherry come home! Sherry come home!" Kristina cried. She took the news to heart, then sighed her relief and fell asleep on the couch, as if to say, "Well, so much for one day."

Mary Matheny, Jody Matheny's younger sister, was staying at the home of an aunt and uncle, Margaret and Jim Lucas. She ran naked out of the bathtub when she heard the family shouting out the news.

"They found Jody!" she screamed, running dripping wet down the hall.

Jean Campbell, Jody's mother, was certain God's will had been done. "God had to have had a hand in their escape!" she exclaimed.

Jim Estabrook was talking to the FBI when he heard the cheering. But the FBI could not immediately confirm the news. They warned Jim not to get too excited yet. After the necessary calls to Alameda County, however, they finally confirmed the reports. The children and Ed Ray were all safe.

Jim felt great, but there was something missing; his son was still not home where he belonged. His wife, Leanna, was thanking God for the children's release.

One family heard the news and got on their knees in the living room, together, to thank God for delivering the children. They never doubted that God was responsible for the children's escape and wanted to "shout it from the housetops" that He had answered their prayers.

Out at the Brown's farmhouse on Avenue 23½, the first report came over the television that ten of the children had been found. That was quickly changed to all of the children as Joan Brown reached for the telephone to call the sheriff's office.

They didn't dare believe until it was confirmed.

When it was, there were tears and relief. Their friend, Pat Handley, was there.

"They're the Lord's children," she remarked. "I sure hope they don't forget who really got them out of this."

Over at Ed Ray's ranch on Avenue 18, there was quite a celebration going on. Relations and friends filled the small farmhouse and spilled out into the back yard. They heard the news on television and let up a cheer they thought could be heard in Madera, a few miles away.

Odessa's faith was beautiful, strong and sure. "I'm sure God sent Edward to be with those children because he is so strong. A weaker man could never have done it."

Carol Marshall looked out the window of her friend Tuffy Smith's house. She had been taking tranquilizers most of the day and had been in an up-and-down frame of mind. When the medicine was working, she was optimistic and cheerful. When it wore off, she was sure her son was dead.

It was getting dark outside. That in itself was depressing. During the day, it hadn't been so bad. News reports of the police efforts up and down the state had kept her going. At least she knew there were people out looking, planes were circling and search parties were combing the area for any possible clues.

But at night, most of the search would have to stop. And the hours of worry would be futile.

Her body was giving in as her emotional and physical strength slowly drained away. "I can't take another night," she whispered weakly. "Not another horrible night like the last one."

The night would be so much harder on the kids, too. It is more frightening for kids to cope with darkness.

Just then, a flash across the screen of the television set snapped her back to reality. She turned abruptly and recognized it as a news bulletin.

Frantic, she leaped over the coffee table to turn up the sound.

"The twenty-six children and their bus driver kidnapped from a school bus in Chowchilla have all been found alive and well in a rock quarry in Livermore. Police now are questioning the children to determine how they escaped from being buried alive there.

"Repeat: The twenty-six children and their bus driver kidnapped. . . ."

"Tuffy!" Carol screamed. In seconds everyone was in the living room. When the bulletin was over, they looked up into each other's dazed eyes, afraid to be excited yet. Could this just be a cruel rumor? So much false information had been floating around, Carol didn't know whose word to trust.

"Tuffy, call the police and see if it's true," she begged.

Smith moved to the phone immediately.

"Yeah, Tuffy Smith. We just heard a report that the kids were found. Is it true?"

He hung up the phone.

"It's true. They found them. They're fine."

The camp counselors at Jackass Rock were becoming more and more concerned about Kandi Marshall. She had not had anything to drink or eat. It was as if she could hear nothing they said. "She's in a trance," they whispered. "Like a vegetable."

Her friends continued to pray, not only for Mike, but also for Kandi. What was going on in her mind? Was she having a nervous breakdown?

Kandi was as confused over her condition as was everyone else. Her mind could concentrate on nothing but her family. And Mike. Would she ever see him again? People and voices were just a vague blur.

A radio report stabbed into her trance like an icy knife.

"We have good news about the twenty-six children and their bus driver who were kidnapped yesterday. They have been found in Alameda County and have been taken to Santa Rita Rehabilitation Center for questioning."

Kandi snapped to attention. Her pale face brightened and she let out a squeal of delight. A rousing cheer and shouts of "praise the Lord" filled the campground.

Her appetite returned with the good news: "I'm starving!"

CHAPTER THIRTEEN

While the parents celebrated, the children were being transferred from the gravel pit. The Alameda County prison transport bus which carried them pulled up in front of the Santa Rita Rehabilitation Center in Livermore. One by one, the little ragamuffins filed out of the bus. They bore little resemblance to the happy children who had left Dairyland School the day before. Their faces were caked with mud, a mixture of the dirt that fell into the van as they made their escape and the tears they couldn't hold back.

Their clothing was ragged, torn and dirty. Some of the younger girls wore the borrowed shirts of the boys over their bathing suits. The stench, a mixture of sweat, urine, mildew and dirt, permeated every inch of the children's bodies.

Their eyes were full of questions about this new and strange place. What would happen to them here? When could they see their mommies and daddies? Many of the eyes struggled to stay open and several children fell asleep as soon as they were seated in the training room of the administration building.

Their hunger was the first thing the staff paid attention to and sandwiches and milk, cake, pie and ice cream were brought in from the mess hall. The children were allowed to eat all they wanted and some of them consumed desserts as if all the bakeries of the world had been outlawed. Jeff Brown alone managed to put away two pieces of cake, three pieces of pie and several ice cream cups. All this, on top of two jumbo hamburgers.

Drs. Howard Wax and George Lejnicks set up a makeshift examining table at one end of the room and with the help of nurse David Johnson checked the children for possible injuries. They treated a variety of cuts and bruises, scratches and bumps, while in the next room the FBI questioned the tired youngsters.

Sherry Hinesley kept falling asleep.

"Sherry, darling, I know you're tired, angel. But we want to talk to you. Can you take your thumb out of your mouth for just a second?" asked one frustrated investigator.

Monica Ardery was scared about the questioning.

"Don't worry," said one of her little friends.

"They ask you a lot of questions and then they give you stuff."

Close-by, in Hayward, Bill Auffarth was watching television in his home when a news bulletin interrupted his viewing: "The twenty-six children and their bus driver kidnapped yesterday from Chowchilla were found this evening in a rock quarry in Livermore. They had been buried alive and dug their way out. They appear to be well and have been taken to Santa Rita Rehabilitation Center for medical examinations and questioning by the FBI."

Auffarth, a nurse at Santa Rita, reached for the phone. He called in and volunteered to help out. Within minutes, he left for the center.

"Anybody here from Chihuahua?" he asked, walking into the room where the children were waiting. From then on, he teased one after another, proposed to several and washed as many faces as he could. Tenderly, he combed and braided six-year-old Stella Carrejo's long, black hair. Her face was dirty and smudged with mud, but her brown eyes looked into his with trust.

The children began to regain their appearances as the dirt came off and smiles appeared. They exchanged their filthy clothing for the white, baggy uniforms usually worn by semi-maximum security prisoners. Ray was fitted with blue coveralls.

An FBI man couldn't resist Jennifer Brown's

big blue eyes and crooked smile. "I'd like to marry this little snaggle-toothed girl," he grinned and she blushed bashfully.

Then, it was time for the children to meet the press, which was waiting anxiously to take the first pictures that would let the world know the children had escaped unharmed.

The children smiled and posed and giggled as reporters and photographers lavished attention on them. Some sat at desks and drew pictures of happy faces.

No one noticed Ed Ray watching the scene from nearby. He hardly looked like a hero and it never occurred to him that he was.

Linda Carrejo clung to nurse Bill as the flashbulbs popped and shyly hid her face in his jacket. This affectionate attention caused Jeff Brown some consternation. Linda had been his girlfriend for some time.

"Are you married?" he demanded of Bill.

"Yes, I am," he replied.

"Are you a Mormon?"

"Huh? A Mormon?"

"Yeah! Are you a Mormon?" Jeff repeated patiently.

"No, I'm not," Bill answered, puzzled at the question.

"That's good," Jeff said, breathing a sigh of relief. "If you were a Mormon, you could have more than one wife."

The children eagerly told the details of their ordeal to curious reporters and nurses.

"The kids told me they were praying," Bill related. "And they told me Ed Ray had spent a great deal of time on his knees. They said he was crying and praying when the oldest boy, Mike Marshall, finally broke through to daylight.

"Now, listen, I believe in God, but I'm not really into it. But when I heard this story, with Ray down there on his knees praying, then they broke through, it was really something . . . like a miracle. . . ."

At last, it was time to head home. The children lined up in front of the red, white and blue Greyhound charter bus. Behind the wheel was driver Walter Cairola. Before they left, the staff at Santa Rita brought out cases of milk, grape and orange juice and crates of apples for the children to take home. They filled their pockets with the fruit to last the long bus ride to Chowchilla. They even stashed a few to take home to parents, brothers and sisters.

The big doors opened and the children boarded the vehicle for their third bus ride in thirty-six hours. It was 1:15 A.M. Saturday, July 17.

Jeff Brown's indomitable sense of humor was not dampened by his circumstances. Slinging a pillowcase full of his belongings over his shoulder, he boarded the bus with a "Ho-ho-ho! Here comes Santa Claus."

Nurse David Johnson and Ed Ray took aisle seats in the center of the bus. Behind the driver was an armed Highway Patrol officer and three women deputies from Alameda County. One carried a gun. Another armed CHP officer rode in the back of the bus. They counted heads several times to be positive everyone was aboard.

The bus slowly pulled out, flanked front and rear by Highway Patrol cars which escorted the precious cargo the 115 miles to anxiously waiting families.

Mike Marshall modestly took a seat in the back and was immediately spotted by two of the older girls, Irene Carrejo and Lisa Barletta, who sat next to him "to keep him warm." Over and over, they called Mike their hero and snuggled up to him. They took plenty of teasing from Bill, who couldn't resist walking back to give some good-natured ribbing.

Finally, the frolicking quieted down as the drone of the bus lulled the exhausted children to sleep.

"Please, Bill, wake us when we get close to Chowchilla."

"Chowchilla? Where's that? We're going to Chewchowchow," he joked.

Stella and Linda Carrejo crawled onto Bill's lap to curl up and sleep.

During the ride, Jennifer Brown woke up twice, screaming, "Leave us alone! Leave us alone!" She slept in a deputy's arms the rest of the way home.

Ed Ray talked all the way home to nurse Johnson about his home and family and the joy of being free. Just knowing he was safe was a great blessing.

During the conversation, he kept watch over his tired flock of children. He walked back through the bus to cover this one with a blanket and to touch that one reassuringly. He and the kids were safe, but his concern did not end until he saw the children in the arms of their parents.

Another man would already have a big head about all of this, Bill thought, as he watched Ed Ray with the children. But this simple man really cares about these kids.

Nurse David listened as the bus driver talked about his fears during their time in the hole. He had prayed time and again for God's help and his prayers were answered. They had escaped their tomb.

And his final prayer was also being granted as the big bus turned left off Robertson Boulevard to pull into the parking lot of the police station. Every child was coming home safe.

The children were wide awake by the time the bus came to a stop. It was 3:52 A.M. Saturday. They had been gone almost exactly thirty-six hours. Through the windows, they could see the bright, glaring television lights and hear the tumultuous cheers of friends and relatives waiting outside.

Jennifer Brown, barefoot and wrapped in an army blanket, was the first one off the bus.

In a matter of minutes, trembling, weeping parents grabbed their children to hold them tight and ask over and over again, "Are you all right?"

Andrea and Larry Park rushed into the waiting arms of their parents. Rodney picked up his daughter and turned to look into the eyes of his father-in-law who only a few hours ago had demanded, "Where is your God now?"

Both men knew what Rodney was thinking before he said it. "If it hadn't been for God, the kids never would have been brought back home," he stated firmly.

Llywellen Clark slowly nodded his head in agreement.

He acknowledged that the children's escape had to be of God. Rodney was amazed.

Margie and Bill Parker clutched their daughter tightly against them. In Margie's hand was Barbara's favorite teddy bear.

Ed Ray made his way through the throng of families, newsmen and friends, astounded at the turnout. He was sure the only people who would be there to meet him at that hour of the morning were the families of the children.

"Don't say a word, Ed. Give the *National Enquirer* an exclusive story and we'll pay you." The rest of the offer was cut off by the screaming crowd. Ray just kept heading for the police station.

"What happened, Ed?"

"Can you tell us how you feel?"

"How'd you get out?"

His wife, Odessa, tears streaming down her face, was waiting for him inside. Her arms went instinctively around his neck and she buried her face in his shoulder.

Ray couldn't hold back his smile. As he typically

reacts to a sentimental situation, Ray joked, "Honey, watch out now. I don't smell too good!"

Odessa couldn't have cared less. That greasy, muddy, sweaty man was the bravest, most fantastic man on earth.

In the midst of this heartwarming scene, John Brown, his voice choking with emotion, walked over to his son and said, "How're you doing, son?"

In a loud voice, which echoed the feelings of parents and children alike, Jeff grinned and said, "Come on, dad. Let's go home."

As they turned to go out the door, it looked like daylight outside because of the blinding lights of television cameras.

Some walked out triumphantly, grinning from ear to ear. Others, in a hurry to go home to mend their torn families, covered their children's heads and hid their faces as they ran the gauntlet of television lights, flashing cameras and microphones stuck into their paths.

"Don't look, honey. Keep your head down," admonished one mother.

"Shut your eyes! Don't open your eyes," yelled another.

Reporters pressed tightly against each other and tripping over wires, equipment and each other, shot out questions:

"How are you feeling, Jennifer?"

"Can you tell us what happened?"

Some of the children, showing a new sophistication for their country way of life, responded: "No comment."

The news media was in a state of calamity. This was the biggest story in years and they couldn't get to Ray.

Each time a member of the police department dared to step out of the building, he was surrounded by newsmen: When is Ray going to talk? Is he coming out today? When will we get his statement? Is everyone all right? Did he say anything?

The police repeatedly told reporters there would be no statement from Ed Ray that day. They wouldn't hear of it.

Undaunted and used to getting the run-around, they stayed, convinced he would talk.

Ed and Odessa sat inside, safe from the turmoil outside. The news media frightened Ray. He had never had any reason to be interviewed before in his life. All those cameras and microphones were as scary to face as the kidnappers. He imagined them firing questions at him faster than he could think. Ed was not an educated man and he was totally out of his element in this situation.

Odessa confronted a newsman. "Okay. If we come out, will you just be quiet and let him tell his story?"

The newsman's expression looked like Christmas morning.

"Mrs. Ray, we will do anything you want."

She looked at her husband. They exchanged a "well, why not?" smile and out the door they came to a barrage of cheering.

Ray held his head down as he began to speak.

Where there once was uncontrolled noise so loud it could be heard down the street, now there was only the whirr of cameras.

The reporters were silent as he spoke, except on three occasions when they burst into cheers as he recounted the story.

When he had poured out all he could remember of the bizarre happenings and answered a few questions, the police abruptly cut off the press conference. They led Ray out, his path again lined with congratulations and praises.

As the Rays were walking down a hall, an insistent reporter broke through the door and came running after them.

Oh boy, a real live one, Ray and Odessa were thinking as they prepared to tell him they had nothing else to say.

"Mr. Ray?" the breathless reporter blurted out.

"Yes?" Ray acknowledged, readying his speech.

"I just want to shake your hand."

In a state of surprise, that easy smile and warm glow that hadn't been seen in a while washed over Ed's face.

Ray put out his hand.

The Chowchilla children were numb and exhausted from their experience, but they woke up to telephone calls and early morning visits from the press.

They hardly knew what to make of their new status as celebrities. At first they were shy before the cameras, but later on, they got the hang of it. And even started to enjoy it.

"Hello, Barbara? I'm from *The New York Times*. I'm sorry to bother you, but could I talk to you for a few minutes?"

"Jeff? Just a few questions from the *Los Angeles Times*."

"Hold it right there, Becky! Good girl! Great shot!"

"Tell us about the escape, Mike. How did you feel while you were down in the hole?"

"I can't get them away from the television," Joan Brown complained of Jeff and Jennifer. "They want to watch every newscast."

The two Brown children, like most of the others, were totally enthralled seeing themselves interviewed on television. They pored over the newspapers to read stories of their escape.

They were even more flattered when the FBI called them in to provide information for the composite photos of the abductors. Jeff and Jennifer's bright, articulate observations delighted reporters and aided police from the beginning.

Their descriptions resulted in an all-points bulletin by the police for three men and two vans.

But the facts of the case still made no more sense than before. Even more mysteries shrouded the biggest, most bizarre kidnapping in the history of the United States.

Jennifer had the problem already analyzed.

"The kidnappers probably had too many toys and not enough love when they were growing up."

Along with the excitement of sudden fame, a swift undercurrent of fear kept the parents on edge.

The kidnappers still were at large. Would they come back to Chowchilla to finish the job they started? Hundreds of crank calls and threats were driving spikes into the hearts of all those involved. One woman called the children repeatedly, warning, "It's not over yet."

"I am more apprehensive now than I have been throughout this whole ordeal," Joan Brown said. "I think I will feel uneasy until they are found."

The possible motives still escape her. "I hate to think it was revenge. There was no rhyme or reason for that. Greed? For money? I don't know which is worse, revenge or greed. But thrill seeking, like some are saying, that shows how distorted some people's thinking really is. If they did it for thrills, then they're sick and our nation must be sick.

"I hope they will come down strong on the kidnappers so the whole nation will realize we are on the wrong track and change. People who make up this nation have rights too. We should get rid of the kooks and nuts."

Evelyn Reynolds still was fearful for her children.

"There is always someone with my children and I have no intention of letting them go anyplace until those men are caught. I think everyone will be more aware of where his children are."

Bill Parker, Barbara's father, stayed home and watched everything that went on in his neighborhood.

"I'm not sleeping with all the threats that have come in since the kids escaped. Those men must be the nearest thing to animals you can find in human beings."

CHAPTER FOURTEEN

Chowchilla awoke Sunday morning as if from three days of one, long, horrible nightmare. Could the incredible horror story which the children told be true?

The streets were deserted during the late morning hours while most of the population attended one or another of this small town's nineteen churches. It was a day to give thanks. They were reverent and relieved as they praised God for bringing their children home from harm.

Mrs. Billy Heffington, mother of ten-year-old Jodie, stood before the congregation at the First United Methodist Church during the special prayer service for her daughter and proclaimed, "As parents of one of the children, we know God answers prayers. Otherwise, we wouldn't have her back."

Beverly Hansen, a member of the church, shared her certainty that God was with the children. She told the congregation how she was led to buy Jeffrey Brown a Bible a year before.

The Rev. Glen Miller acknowledged God's hand in bringing the children home safely during his morning sermon. "God has given us a great victory in His justice and goodness," Miller said.

His message was based on Romans 13: "Therefore he who resists and sets himself up against the authorities resists what God has appointed and arranged—in divine order. And those who resist will bring down judgment upon themselves—receiving the penalty due them" (verse 2, Amplified Version).

Just four blocks down from the police station, Pastor John Surratt of the First Assembly of God Church was praising God for the miracle escape. "I give all the credit to our living Lord who brought them home," he said. "It is a shame Chowchilla has been recognized in the way it has, but it is one of the cities that now has been seen across the world." Pastor Surratt made special mention of bus driver Ed Ray and suggested he received divine inspiration during his captivity.

Spontaneous responses of clapping, "Hallelujah" and "yes, yes," added spirit and confirmation to Surratt's message. The congregation maintained that verve and more as they swayed to the rhythm of a popular hymn, their arms lifted up in praise.

> Count your many blessings,
> Name them one by one;
> Count your many blessings,
> See what God hath done.

The Rev. Dwight Robertson, the church's youth pastor, illustrated how God stepped in to take control of the situation. "Do you realize," he said, "that we could be hearing today the report of a multiple funeral? But instead, mothers and fathers are smiling.

"That's what it's all about—divine intervention."

The rescue, Robertson said, was a direct answer to the prayers lifted up in an ecumenical church service Friday afternoon and in homes across the country. "The prayers were answered," he stated. "We prayed and God intervened."

Among the joyous voices in the congregation were Ted and Tine Zylstra and their seven-year-old daughter, Sandy, who was the last child to get off the bus before it was hijacked.

Even though every child was brought home safe, a residual fear in the city put Sunday school attendance at the Cathedral of Faith, an Assembly of God Church, at an all time low. Drivers arrived at the church with near-empty buses, explaining to the Rev. Jerry Burns that the parents were afraid to let their children ride the bus.

However, Janice and Rodney Park and their children, Andrea and Larry, went eagerly to church. They couldn't miss this special opportunity to thank God for blessing them with safe, healthy children.

Despite her knowledge that the terror was over, Andrea could not break away from her parents long enough to attend her Sunday school class. Instead, she clung to her mother during the church service.

The Browns decided to attend the First Baptist Church. Really, Jeff and Jennifer decided. They had been attending alternately the First United Methodist Church and the First Baptist. But, the Baptist Church had had the prayer vigil Friday afternoon and the Browns wanted the congregation to see the result of their prayers.

It was a joyful service and one filled with praise and thanksgiving to the living God who brought the children home. At one point, John Brown, a man of few words, rose to tell the people, "We'd like to thank the Lord for bringing our children home."

The Rev. R. S. Buskirk, like other pastors around town, singled out Ed Ray for special praise. "How I thank God that we had a man like Ed Ray with these little children to love and comfort them."

Rev. Buskirk talked of the intervention of God through prayer and the hand of God present during the ordeal. His lesson was taken from Matthew 27:46 where Jesus, hanging on the cross, questioned, "My God, my God, why hast thou forsaken me?" He related the Scripture to the questioning of parents and residents of Chowchilla who asked God why the kidnapping had taken place. "It is good for an individual to ask questions of the Deity. The Deity Himself asked questions like this. . . ."

Throughout the service Joan Brown remained thoughtful and contemplative. So much had happened these last few days and this feeling that God was trying to get through to her kept her stomach churning.

The service was nearly over when Rev. Buskirk began the final prayer.

"Examine yourself to see where you stand with God, what direction you're going. Is there an emptiness, a void that needs to be filled?"

I just can't, Lord, Joan was thinking. I haven't the courage to live your way and I'm so afraid if I accepted your Son that it wouldn't stay with me. I've been baptized twice and it didn't take.

". . . all heads are bowed and all eyes are closed," the pastor was saying, "and if you feel you want to make some changes in your life, this is the time to ask Jesus Christ to come into your heart as your Savior.

"And to seal that commitment, just raise your hand. . . ."

Somebody will see, she thought panicking; I can't do it. Her heart was beating madly. I want to, she thought, I don't know if I have the courage. I haven't even talked to the minister and I don't think I can do it.

Fight as she might, her hand went up. The struggle was over.

CHAPTER FIFTEEN

Fear, Joy . . . And Questions

The precious hijacked cargo is home and nothing else seems nearly as important.

The twenty-six youngsters from the Chowchilla area—and their sturdy and solicitous companion, bus driver Frank Edward Ray Jr.—have had a little time to recover from their abduction and bizarre imprisonment by three armed and masked men.

They will need time. Children are resilient, but twenty-eight hours of uncertainty and terror—starting with their forced removal from their school bus and ending with their escape from a buried van in a quarry near Livermore—are bound to leave a residue of fear.

Our hearts go out to their parents, who had

their own agony to cope with during the long vigil. Now they will have to reassure—and keep reassuring—their boys and girls that the world is not all that threatening a place. Even if they have their private doubts.

In the meantime, as the hunt for the abductors continues, there are the endless questions. What was the motive? Was a message—ransom, extortion, whatever—going to be delivered to authorities, and if so, what prevented it? Why did the masked men ask each child's name and age—to establish proof of captivity? Why did they apparently abandon their captives to unbearable entombment? Would they have returned?

Why did they choose a rural school district in Central California as their target? How carefully did they check the bus route and rehearse the abduction? Were they in fact outsiders?

It is a measure of our time that the speculation during those terrible hours between Thursday evening and Friday night included fear that a big-city mass murderer—the so-called Zodiac killer—had extended his reach, or that political terrorists wanted to trade innocent children for prisoners.

In the last few decades there have been many painful vigils which have attracted journalistic attention from all over the world. Men trapped in submarines. A child caught in an abandoned well. Miners cut off by cave-ins. Hostages captured by terrorists. Children kidnapped from wealthy parents for ransom.

Some had happy endings; too many did not.

But at least those events were comprehensible, if no less awful.

The Chowchilla abduction makes no sense. Not yet. Not until those responsible are caught. It can't happen too soon.

For now, though, we can extend a hand to those whose ordeal can only be imagined—the stolen children and the parents who wept tears of worry and grief, and finally joy. May the fears subside with merciful swiftness.

The Fresno Bee, July 19, 1976

Even with the prayers of millions, it may take years for the children to shed the scars of the experience.

The parents, too, are nursing their own wounds. They want to forget, but the painful remembrance looks across the breakfast table at them every morning.

At night, there is no rest. Parents are awakened to kiss away tears of terror from children who, alas, cannot forget either.

Like some of the others, Johnny Estabrook still has trouble sleeping. The first night he came home he couldn't sleep at all. He was scared to death they were coming back, he told his father.

"Sometimes he wakes up screaming, thinking they are coming in the back door to get him," Jim Estabrook explained.

Janice Park said neither of her children, Larry and Andrea, could sleep alone after the ordeal.

Janice slept with them while husband Rodney worked nights, but the arrangement just didn't work out.

"I wasn't sleeping and they weren't sleeping," she said, "so I asked the kids, 'If we get a dog, will you sleep in your own beds?' They said yes."

When television newsman Bob Long of Channel 24, KMJ-TV in Fresno, heard of their fears, he arranged for the family to adopt a friendly watchdog, Louie. It was trust at first sight and the children returned to their rooms.

Evelyn Reynolds was forced to quit her job on the graveyard shift at a Chowchilla convalescent hospital when her daughters, Judy and Becky, started having violent nightmares.

Dreams disappear by morning, but more lasting conflicts—conceit, jealous schoolmates, delicate egos, nervousness riding the school bus, withdrawal, misbehavior—still remain.

The children are not the only ones with nightmares plaguing their sleep. Ed Ray awoke in the night shortly after he and the children arrived back in Chowchilla. He was sobbing, as the bottled-up emotion finally found release. He dressed and walked for nearly an hour in the fields behind his house, tearfully pouring out the terror and frustration he had kept tightly inside.

In northern California, Dr. Nicholas Cummings, chief psychiatrist for Kaiser-Permanente Foundation, said shortly after the kidnapping that the experience could affect some of the children for years. "Some will come out of it totally unscathed. Others will have future phobias and anxieties. For some it will be a feather in their cap, a way of living.

"The majority will get over it," he said. "A lot depends on experiences prior to this. The kidnapping could be a catalyst for all kinds of mental health problems."

Dr. Max Brannan, a child psychologist in nearby Merced, predicted that the very youngest children probably would be the first to get over the experience.

"Those who are eight, nine and ten years old will retain it longer," he said.

And then, there is Jody Matheny, who carries his Braille typewriter to school each day. The doctors are still checking on the damage to his eyes since the kidnapping. After being a bit of a hero, Jody finds it difficult to accept that someday he will be totally blind.

"Mama," he askes hopefully, "Do you think my eyes will ever get better if I don't strain them a lot? I'd like them to get really, really good like the Six Million Dollar Man. . . ."

Certainly, the parents have been affected by the nightmare.

Although Bob Marshall appeared to have taken the whole predicament calmly and in stride, his standing in the rodeo circuit has subsequently fallen sharply. At the time of the kidnapping, Marshall was tearing up all competition and was 5,000 points ahead of his nearest rival.

Three months later, he was 2,000 points behind the leader.

At least one wounded relationship was healed as a result of the kidnapping. During the time the children were missing, John Brown III got a call from his father in Taft, expressing concern and worry. "John and his father have never been close and his parents haven't been in our home the thirteen years we've been married," Joan Brown explained.

When the children escaped and were reunited with their families, the Browns made a trip to Taft the next weekend. Then, John Brown, Jr. and his wife came to Chowchilla for "Ed Ray and Children Day," a celebration held August 22 honoring the kidnap victims. "We are thrilled to be here," grandfather Brown said at the picnic following the parade down Robertson Boulevard. "Since the kidnapping, the kids have found new grandparents," Joan said softly.

Overnight, Ed Ray became a national folk hero. Letters poured in from all over the country praising his courage, his sense of reponsibility, his heroic deeds. He received letters from people he held in awe: California Gov. Edmund G. Brown, Jr., President Ford, and other well-known personalities.

And now people were holding him in awe. He didn't understand. He has always been a simple man, and fame only makes him feel awkward.

Awards and honors, plaques and citations, gifts and more gifts, were heaped upon him. Yet he has managed to remain modest and unaffected.

There are two funds set up in his name in Chowchilla, one for college scholarships for the children and one for his retirement. Another, a trust fund for the children until they each turn eighteen, has been set up by the Buena Park, California, Lions Club.

Concern for his safety brought gifts that protect his ranch house: a burglar alarm and fire alarm system, a German Shepherd attack dog, Buddy, shipped from North Carolina. The donor was a trainer there who had read about Odessa's fear of possible repercussions from the kidnappers.

Despite the fact that those traumatic thirty-six hours in July brought townspeople closer together, they would like to erase the questionable notoriety it brought to their town. Chowchilla has become a household name around the world.

They are weary of publicity, the newspaper and magazine articles, the television broadcasts, and the attention which they view as an intrusion on their lives.

Most of the people in this tiny town live here because it is so small and they have a chance to escape the problems of life in the big city or the suburbs. They would like life to return to normal—the sooner the better.

There is almost as wide a range of religious experiences as emotional ones. Families flocked to church immediately after the children came home, but months later, attendance dropped off.

For some, the kidnapping resulted in a new commitment to God. Sam Barletta returned to church after forty years. Sherry Hinesley attended mass every day for weeks after she returned home. The Marshalls, among others, started to church for the first time.

Others, like Bill Parker, could not see what part God had played in the children's escape. "I wish I could believe that way. I admire people who have that much faith. But I can't. I believe in God, but that's it. He's never shown me that He is real and working," Bill said.

Rodney Park has seen a significant change in their lives. "Not only have we drawn closer to God, but we have drawn closer as a family. We loved our family before, but there's just something there now that wasn't there before. The kids rarely get on our nerves. They used to be on our nerves constantly. My wife is a very high strung person.

"But since this happened, she has more patience with the children. She hardly ever raises her voice to them and never spanks them.

"In fact, I think they are getting a little spoiled."

"It really shows you," Janice Park added, "and not just us as parents, but everybody that knows, that there's no way those kids and Mr. Ray could have gotten out of that hole under their own strength.

"I really think the kids had been put down there to die and had they found them, even the next day, it would have been too late. It was too well hidden.

"I feel so much closer to God through this. I have rededicated my life to Him," Janice said.

Now more than ever before, the parents have drawn together to share one another's burdens. New friendships have blossomed and concern and helping hands have reached across the chasm of pain and despair. They overlook their own woes in order to help those near to them.

Judy Hinesley, who is under heavy medication for severe asthma, also has to fight allergy problems in her children, Sherry and Kristina.

"But we only have allergy problems here. We can still function normally. Jody Matheny takes his Braille typewriter to school every day. I really feel sorry for him."

She looked down at her daughter playing Monopoly on the floor.

"If only the money in that game were real. . . ."

Another child, Larry Park, is hyperactive and other families have expressed concern for how the kidnapping will affect him.

"He has taken it in stride for the most part," his mother, Janice Park, said. She looked down at the needlepoint sampler she was working on.

"A man, Don Foster, sent this to Mayor Dumas.

I cried when I read it and I just had to do something special with it."

It reads simply:

"They were only a breath of a nation, yet overnight they became the heart of the world."

EPILOGUE

Two weeks after the kidnapping, three men were charged with forty-five counts of kidnapping, kidnapping with bodily harm and robbery. They are Frederick Newhall Woods, twenty-four; James Schoenfeld, twenty-four, and his brother, Richard, twenty-two.

John and Joan Brown, their faces still drawn from the agony of the previous three days, were in church Sunday morning to give thanks for the safe return of their children, Jeff, ten, and Jennifer, eight.

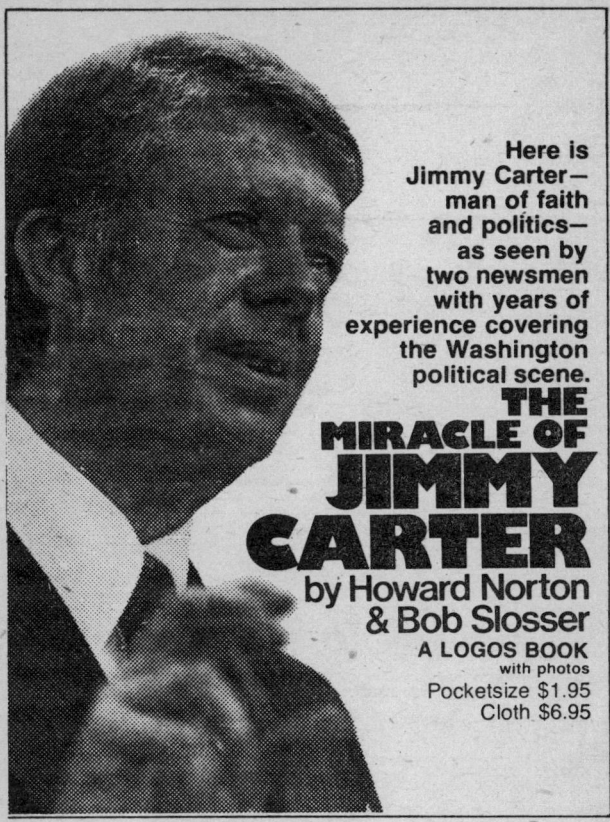

Here is Jimmy Carter— man of faith and politics— as seen by two newsmen with years of experience covering the Washington political scene.

THE MIRACLE OF JIMMY CARTER

by Howard Norton & Bob Slosser

A LOGOS BOOK
with photos
Pocketsize $1.95
Cloth $6.95

Logos International Fellowship
201 Church Street
Plainfield, N.J. 07060

NAME _____
STREET _____
CITY _____ STATE _____ ZIP _____

(Prices are subject to change without notice)

Keep in touch with world-wide religious news and trends—
Read—
THE NATIONAL COURIER,
a bi-weekly newspaper and
LOGOS JOURNAL,
a bi-monthly magazine.

Send $1.00 for sample copies of both.
NC/LJ Trial Samples
201 Church Street
Plainfield, N.J. 07060

Name _____

Address _____

City _____

State _____ Zip _____

For a catalog of other fine inspirational books, write:

WBS Catalog
Box 292
Watchung, N.J. 07061

Name _____
Address_____
City _____
State_____Zip_____

☐ Send free inspirational catalog

KIDNAPPED!

The bus was empty.

There were some towels, a few school papers, and a piece of ceramic artwork—the relics of a busload of happy children who only a few hours before were on their way home from school. Now they were gone. Twenty-six children, ages five to fourteen, had simply disappeared.

What really happened during those fearful thirty-six hours before the children were once again in the arms of their parents? What faith sustained them during the hours they were buried alive in an abandoned quarry? How did a stricken community find fresh faith in the midst of catastrophe? Here is the remarkable true story.

P217/$1.95
LOGOS INTERNATIONAL
Plainfield, N.J. 07060